THE TENANT FARMER'S SON

It's Not Where You End Up in Life, It's How Far You've Come

RONALD E. HENDERSON, MD

Copyright © 2015 by Ronald E. Henderson, Twin Valley Press

All rights reserved.
Printed in the United States of America.

Library of Congress Cataloging-in-Publication applied for.
ISBN: 978 0 692-47340-5

Disclaimer: This life story does not represent a factual work
of nonfiction but the autobiographical account of the life of
Ronald E. Henderson.

On the cover: Hanging behind me in the portrait is the
crosscut saw my father and I used to cut trees for firewood
and fence posts. The book in my hand represents the value
my parents and my wife, Beth, and I place on learning
and education. Including the family clock is a nod to the
importance of remembering our roots.—REH

Edited by Haden Holmes Brown
and designed by Dana Ezzell Gay
of *A Past Preserved*

www.apastpreserved.com

Printed by Gorham Printing
Centralia, Washington

THE TENANT FARMER'S SON

It's Not Where You End Up in Life, It's How Far You've Come

RONALD E. HENDERSON, MD

Beth Ann Summerville, 1955.

For My Beth

CONTENTS

Drs. Ronald E. Henderson and Frank O. Page, St. Vincent's Hospital, 2002.

FOREWORD

Thirty years ago, I had the privilege of beginning my professional career in Birmingham at St. Vincent's Hospital with Dr. Ronald E. Henderson. Ron was regarded as one of the premier practicing physicians in the city and the state. His work ethic and unflagging determination recall the heroes of the faith mentioned in Hebrews 12. He encouraged all of us to "run the race with endurance." I was ready for that; however, I was totally unprepared for the challenge, intensity, and plain fun that ensued.

Ron is a self-starter and has the capacity on any day and at any time to *just do the work*. A true professional, he came to work every single day of his career as if he felt absolutely wonderful; he never allowed personal issues to detract from the task at hand. He had one work mode, and that was full-throttle drive and focus. With amazing stamina, Ron could outwork all of us! His energy and enthusiasm were infectious.

Our practice started surgery each morning at 6:30 a.m. because Ron wanted to start seeing patients in the office at 8 a.m. That meant we began hospital rounds *before* surgery, at about 4:30 a.m. In surgery, Ron and I often assisted each other, and as a skillful surgeon, he was efficient. His expectations of those around him were high, so the nurses and staff were prepared. We also operated from noon–2 p.m. because the office was closed during lunchtime, and we were back in the office seeing patients from 2 p.m.–5 p.m. Every third night, one of us was on call to deliver babies and slept at the hospital. That was our typical day. And since we all liked to work hard, it was fun.

In 1985, our practice had three physicians and twenty staff. Over the years, the practice grew to nineteen physicians and 150 staff in eight offices. Staff meetings were important to recognize and thank staff; Ron was appropriately generous with praise. As a manager, he was firm but fair. Part of Ron's strength was to recognize and hire talent. He also engaged the best advisors for our practice, such as top accountants, attorneys, and insurance professionals. When we met, it was a "Who's Who" of Birmingham, an impressive group.

I will always be grateful for Ron's leadership and for the special perspective of patient care he inspired at St. Vincent's Hospital and in our state. Above all, he was committed to treating the whole patient. In those early years, ob-gyns were usually the patients' primary physicians. Part of what made Ron uniquely suited to this role was his training and experience. In his era of medical training, students were exposed to a wider range of care instead of focusing on areas of specialty. Ron had also experienced two years of general practice in a small town, where he was in the trenches, completely on his own. He developed this wonderful grasp of taking care of the patient from head to toe. He had that extra sensibility to assess and treat patients by looking at them; he was not one to overreact and order fourteen tests or put them in the hospital. If needed, Ron would make an "appropriate referral" as he called it. Ron's experience, his cognitive skills, and his inquisitiveness made him comfortable treating the whole patient. And, as Ron would also say, "Take care of the patient, and the patient will take care of you," meaning that they will come back for care and will refer others to you.

Ron had thousands of devoted patients whom he'd seen for most of their adult lives. They respected him as an excellent clinician; they'd say, "Dr. Henderson told me to do this, I'm gonna do this." His direct style conveyed that he was very certain about what the patient should do. He presented a firm plan, with challenges such as exercise and weight loss. Ron always chided patients pretty hard about their weight! But you know what? He effected change. You'd have a few patients who would change physicians because "he got onto me." But Ron could take the heat; he didn't mind confrontation. And that carried through to his managerial role—confrontation was not bad, it was working through things. Ron's former patients still ask about him.

Ron had such a self-assured, compassionate way of dealing with patients, they accepted whatever he told them, often without question. On one remarkable occasion, Ron and I operated simultaneously on patients of the same name. Following the two very different surgeries, I went to the assigned waiting room and quickly realized I was talking to Ron's patient's family. I went to the other waiting room to address the family of my patient and they said that I need not bother, that Dr. Henderson had already come in and told them how surgery went, and all was fine. They had never seen Ron but totally accepted what he told them about the wrong operation.

Much of Ron's success can be attributed to his innate skill as a communicator, his ability to describe complex ideas with unusual clarity. This talent extends to his writing and public speaking efforts. In group settings, Ron builds trust, respect, unity, and relationships. I have known him as a partner in medicine, board member, teacher, mentor, educator, committee chair, parent, and friend. In all these roles, he tapped into an understanding of people that allowed for the free flow of ideas and an exchange of constructive criticism.

Ron's strength as a communicator also helped him sell his progressive ideas. As a visionary, he saw medical and entrepreneurial innovations in the "big picture," not in small increments. You have to work to stay current. Ron would read about a new trend or a new medical technique or management style, and he would implement it. His foresight in the early years led to the advancement of new ideas such as the mindset that the physician who is more efficient, reduces waste, and lowers costs is actually a higher quality physician for the patient. He refused to tolerate excesses, such as physicians ordering too many tests or resorting to hospitalization too quickly. He worked to *shorten* the length of patient stay in the hospital, achieving better outcomes and saving health-care dollars. In the mid-1970s, Ron introduced innovations such as allowing fathers in the delivery rooms and offering epidurals.

Ron Henderson has been a cornerstone in medicine and in our specialty for many years, not only in his efforts to meet the needs of patients but also in training residents and inspiring the careers of countless Alabamians in health care. He has helped improve health care in our state by serving on state and local boards and within educational institutions and hospitals.

REH, as we called him in the '80s and '90s, has worn many hats during his dynamic career in medicine. In retirement, he has again set an example for all of us, as one who has "stayed on journey." He continues to find meaningful ways to use his talents and vast store of knowledge. Without a doubt, health care in Alabama has been shaped by the intentions and convictions of Ronald E. Henderson. His impact on health will continue to reverberate throughout the city, state, and country for generations to come.

I am personally grateful that God has used Ron as an exemplary role model, valued mentor, fair critic, encourager, goal setter, and teacher in my life. He is truly a person who lives by the Golden Rule, treating others as he wishes to be treated. I have cherished his influence and friendship over the years more than my words might convey.

REH, thank you for your endless hours of work and for encouraging others to serve in health care.

—Frank O. Page MD, FACOG
Past OB-GYN Department Chair and Chief of Staff, St. Vincent's Hospital
Partner, Page, Hudson & Taylor, Gynecology at St. Vincent's

Beth Summerville Henderson, 1997.

PREFACE

The Lord sent a wonderful woman, Beth Summerville Henderson, to be my bride. Beth has been an incredible wife over the past fifty-seven years and contributed in many ways to the endeavors of which you are about to read in this book. This compassionate, competent, Christian woman is equally responsible for our mutual success—a full partner. Beth has acted as my soul mate, my cheerleader, and my compass.

From the beginning, Beth and I have trusted each other and never doubted that our marriage was going to be for life. We watched many of our med school classmates "fall in lust" and yet never fall in love; seven years out, they were having affairs and getting divorced. That never crossed our minds. In addition to a strong attraction, we were bonded by common goals, Christian morals, and a mutual respect—the keystones of a successful marriage. An essential coping skill that has kept us together is our ability to get beyond the "flashpoints" that occur in every marriage. A conflict will inevitably arise; but then we back off, allow some cooling time to gain perspective, and then sit down to resolve the issue. And we do that beautifully.

As my compass, Beth has made sure I was headed in the right direction, for the right reasons. She consistently exercises good judgment—Beth has common sense seeping out of every pore. She is able to take four or five factors, weigh them, prioritize them, and make a solid decision. Occasionally, I have a few grandiose ideas, and she talks me out of them. She's kept me out of the ditches for the most part!

Together we have made the pivotal decisions that have determined our path. When I succumb to "second-guessing" a decision, Beth says, "You could-have, should-have, ought-to-have done that, but you can't go back." She reminds me that I've "already jumped off the bridge" and that I've got to land. She assures me that beating myself over the head with the misfires is a waste of time, which is good advice.

Because of my aggressive nature, if I see something that needs to be addressed, verbally or directly, I do it without hesitation. Beth does not like confrontation. Her personality is just as smooth as silk. She tells me, "You don't have a filter between your mouth and your brain." So sometimes she helps me temper my presentation. But it doesn't matter if she agrees with me or not, she's going to support me. She's always got my back.

More than anyone else I know, Beth actively lives by the tenets of Christianity, compassion, and caring in her everyday life. She demonstrates to those around her that she cares for and loves them, without any strings attached. My parents adored Beth. Daddy particularly felt close to her and she to him. On two separate occasions, Beth has tenderly nursed me back to health from critical health situations. During those stressful times, her unwavering commitment had a huge influence on my getting well.

Beth not only has a charitable heart but also tremendous capacity. She is able to host a house full of people, the result of seamless advanced planning and implementation. She enjoys people, so she entertains beautifully, making everyone feel comfortable and welcome. As I worked the long hours in medical school, built my practice, and founded four companies, Beth was the parent always there for the kids. When one of our kids stepped out of line, she would pitch it to me to be the disciplinarian. But Beth handled the daily heavy lifting of parenting almost entirely on her own. Even now, when the children are grown, they call Beth for advice, which is all right by me. Our three children could not be any closer to us as parents. The grandchildren call *me* for advice, because I'm "Papa" and I love on 'em, and tell 'em how proud I am of them!

I can easily outline Beth's attributes, but there is an intangible part of her that is harder to describe. She is attractive, loving, and self-reliant—but at the core, I think she can best be described as grounded. When we're getting dressed to go somewhere, I'll ask her, "What do you think I ought to wear?" She *never* asks me that! She has the attitude, *What you see is what you get.* Such inner confidence is rare; I certainly don't have it. She has a strong sense of self, which I attribute to her upbringing. Her parents adored her, which helps instill a positive self-image and strong self-esteem in a young woman. Beth's grounded nature has helped me to approach each situation intellectually and not emotionally.

The magnetism between Beth and me is as strong as ever. We simply enjoy spending time together, which is not always the case for married couples. We *love* to be together. Again, I harken back to the importance of mutual trust, mutual respect, and common goals. I love her dearly. Some days, I tell her four or five times how much I love her. I ask her, "Does it ever bother you that I tell you so often?" And she says, "No, I *love* hearing it."

So as you read the following pages, know that without my Beth by my side, we would not have enjoyed all the successes that have been ours.

—REH

THE TENANT FARMER'S SON

RONALD EARL HENDERSON
FAMILY TREE

JAMES "ELBERT" HENDERSON, FARMER
B. 28 Aug 1887, Aurora, Etowah, AL
D. 24 Aug 1973, Prattville, Autauga, AL

WILLIAM "EARL" HENDERSON, FARMER
B. 27 Oct 1911, Boaz, Etowah, AL
D. 20 Feb 1987, Prattville, Autauga, AL

JESSIE ORA SMITH
B. 22 Feb 1886, GA
D. 29 Nov 1955, Prattville, Autauga, AL

RONALD EARL HENDERSON
B. 28 Jul 1937, Prattville, Autauga, AL

GEORGE T. DILLARD, FARMER
B. 1 Jan 1880, Jordan, Coosa, AL
D. 9 May 1964, Prattville, Autauga, AL

SARA ELLEN DILLARD
B. 12 Aug 1917, Deatsville, Elmore, AL
D. 11 May 1997, Prattville, Autauga, AL

EULA D. PENTON
B. 21 Oct 1882, AL
D. 12 May 1931, Deatsville, Elmore, AL

WILLIAM PRESTON HENDERSON, FARMER
B. 25 Jul 1860, Cherokee County, AL
D. 13 Feb 1925, Short Creek, Etowah, AL

SUSAN "SUDIE" REBECCA HOLCOMB
B. 27 Dec 1869, Etowah County, AL
D. 6 Jun 1951, Short Creek, Etowah, AL

JOHN ASBURY SMITH, REVEREND and FARMER
B. 1 Jan 1839, Hall County, GA
D. 18 Aug 1910, Aurora, Etowah, AL

MARTHA "MARY" ELIZABETH LIPSCOMB
B. abt 1845, GA
D. abt 1887, GA

SAMUEL PINKNEY DILLARD, FARMER
B. 10 Feb 1842, Talladega, AL
D. 11 Sept 1900, Jordan, Coosa, AL

MARTHA ELLEN FERGUSON
B. 6 Oct 1853, Jordan, Coosa, AL
D. 18 Jun 1932, Jordan, Coosa, AL

ABNER JOSEPH PENTON, FARMER
B. 1856 Coosa, AL
D. 1930 Verbena, Chilton, AL

MARTHA SARAH PARTRIDGE
B. 1858 Coosa, AL
D. 8 Jun, 1940, Verbena, Chilton, AL

Opposite far left, William Earl and Sara Dillard Henderson, 1936. *Opposite top,* James Elbert and Jessie Ora Smith Henderson, 1951. *Opposite bottom,* George T. and Eula Penton Dillard, circa 1902. *Above top,* William Preston and Sudie Holcomb Henderson and grandchildren; William Earl Henderson, on front row, right, circa 1918. *Above center:* from left: George Thomas Dillard, Ernest Irvin Dillard, Samuel Pinkney Dillard, Martha Ellen Ferguson Dillard, and Lula Rumicia Dillard, 1899. *Left,* Martha Sara Partridge and Abner Joseph Penton, circa 1920.

Top, Henderson Family, circa 1911, Short Creek, Etowah, AL. From left, seated, Sudie Rebekah Holcomb Henderson holding Irene, James Elbert Henderson holding Beatrice Ophelia, Jessie Ora Smith Henderson holding William Earl. Standing, far left, second row, William Preston Henderson.

Bottom, Dillard Family, circa 1910. From left, Joe Dillard astride oxen. Standing, George T. Dillard, Eula Penton Dillard, others unknown. Front row, Ruby Dillard and Maudie Dillard.

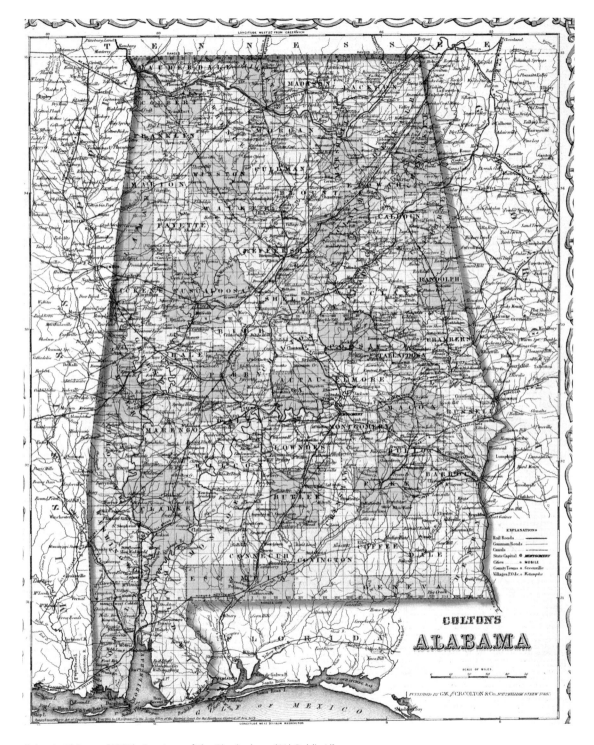

Colton's Alabama (1881), Courtesy of the Birmingham (AL) Public Library.

Top, Family of James Elbert and Jesse Ora Smith Henderson, 1919: Front row, left: William Earl, Grace Callen, James Edward, Jewell Bell. Middle, left: Jessie Ora, James Elbert. Back row: Beatrice Ophelia. (Elbert Preston "Buddy" not yet born). *Bottom left,* Maury McWilliams, Papa Henderson's partner and owner of Prattville drugstore. *Bottom right,* Buddy, Earl, and James at homeplace, about 1936.

CHAPTER 1

PROVING OUR METTLE

James Elbert "Papa" Henderson, my paternal grandfather, was an overseer—he rode a horse and carried a pistol and a whip. In the early 1920s in Marengo County, Alabama, though they were not slaves, black men worked to cut the timber and drag it out. Papa Henderson managed these men. Around 1925, he moved the family north to a farm near Prattville, Alabama, where he had a different type of arrangement. Maury McWilliams, who owned a Prattville drugstore, hired him to operate his 350-acre farm and deeded over half to Papa as upfront payment. The farm was on the west side of Highway 31, north of Prattville, and had six tenant houses on the property. Papa and the tenant farmers ran four teams of plow mules to farm cotton. The eldest male of six children, my daddy, William Earl Henderson, worked alongside him on the farm.

Earl was a handsome young man with a perfectly chiseled nose balancing his large head. He stood about 5'11" and was extremely strong. He later told stories about how, when he was younger, he was "quite the man" and was rarely challenged. In 1929, Daddy graduated with honors from Sydney Lanier High School in Montgomery. He could have gone to college for about $300, but it was the start of the Great Depression, and his family simply didn't have the money. Instead, for the next two years, he would travel to Boaz, Alabama, pick up a cousin, and hitchhike or hop train cars to the panhandle of Texas and to Oklahoma to do migrant farm work for months at a time. He was ashamed of this lowly work, but to me it was a sign of strength and character.

On February 12, 1936, he married my mother, Sara Ellen Dillard. Sara was the fifth child in a family of six and the youngest girl. Her mother, Eula D. Penton Dillard, died of a chronic disease when Sara was twelve years old. She and her brothers had a difficult time for several years after. Her daddy, George T. Dillard, was an uneducated, rough, and callous man. In her teens, my mother moved in with her brother Joe Dillard and his wife, Marie, in Prattville. She was happy there, and in many ways it saved her.

The early challenges in Sara's life molded her into a proud, independent individual. She was working at the local five-and-dime store when she met Daddy. He was twenty-four years old and mother was eighteen when, as a married couple, they moved into a tenant house on Papa's farm and Daddy again worked the land with his father. I was born on July 28, 1937, their firstborn.

That next year, a 116-acre farm, just across Highway 31 from Papa's place, came up for sale through a federal program. The program was designed to get young couples successfully farming land that they could ultimately own. For the first five years, from 1938–1943, my parents had to prove that they could make a living farming the land. Only then would they qualify to take on a mortgage for the property. Daddy had gone to a city school, but he'd had a lifetime of farming experience. It was a serious gamble. I was nine months old when we moved onto our own place.

Left, George T. Dillard, Ron's maternal grandfather.
Right, Eula Dee Penton Dillard, Ron's maternal grandmother.

Top left, Sara and Ronald E. "Ronny" Henderson, 1937. *Top right,* Earl, Sara, and Ronny on their own land in 1937. *Bottom left,* Ronny sporting a hat on the front porch of the new home, 1938. *Bottom right,* Ronny and his rocking chair, 1938.

Those first five years were extremely tough. Daddy cut trees, moved rocks, and filled in holes to ready the fields for crops. He built fences and dug irrigation ditches. He was able to make a go of it in large part because he established friendships with the neighbors and local business people. He had very little money for operations, but his relationships in town allowed him to buy supplies and groceries on credit. Part of the meager income we had during that startup period came from raising sorghum cane and making sorghum syrup with two neighbors. The "egg money" allowed us to buy such staples as sugar, salt, and pepper. The main source of income would come from the harvest of cotton and corn. My parents gradually acquired milk cows and two mules, Jack and Sam, and built the barns.

One of my earliest memories was the night that my mother went into labor with my brother, Gerald Eugene "Jerry" Henderson, in 1940. We were staying with Mama and Papa Henderson, and I was sleeping in a back bedroom. Until then the center of my parents' world, I felt totally abandoned when Mother left me. The pain continued when she brought home a squally baby a couple days later—my life changed forever. Aside from that, I remember my childhood as a very happy time. My brother Thomas "Tommy" Elbert Henderson, nine years my junior, came along much later, in 1946.

Left, Jerry and Ronny, 1943. *Right,* Ronny on sacks of seed on the porch at Papa Henderson's homeplace, 1943.

My family was a working unit that did everything together. We worked the cotton together, tended the garden together, and canned our food together. We were a true team. Mother was the primary caregiver and homemaker but worked alongside Daddy in the fields when the need arose. Standing only 5'2", she was a powerhouse in a small package. In the absence of modern day conveniences, she was up before daylight and still working, without complaint, when the children went to bed. Daddy worked from dawn to dark as well. He had a strong and disciplined work ethic, a workaholic. He always treated me as a partner in the business and gave me a lot of responsibility and latitude. Daddy usually had a cigarette in his hand, and his fingers were always stained with nicotine. In the early days, he'd use Prince Albert tobacco (which he pronounced "'baccer") in a can, which he rolled in cigarette papers. Later, he smoked Lucky Strikes without filters. Daddy wasn't very talkative except when we had company; then he'd talk everybody's ears off.

In 1943, my family was cleared to purchase the land on a forty-year note at a three percent annual interest rate. By the end of that five-year period, they ended up with about twenty cows, twelve acres of cotton, and thirty acres of corn. World War II was on and liquidity was a problem. My parents, along with most everyone else, bought their groceries on credit and settled up in the fall after the cotton and corn were sold. The annual mortgage payment also came due in the fall, and I remember Mother and Daddy strategizing how to raise the $164.39 payment. Somehow, they always managed it. Everybody in the family was impressed that Daddy, at age thirty, owned land—it was a mark of success.

The federal program also provided a brand new four-room house, painted white and situated on concrete pillars. Across the front of the house stretched a thirty-foot-long porch with latticed two-by-four column supports at intervals. On the right side of the porch were the steps leading to the front door. On the opposite side of the house, there was a small screened-in porch that included a pantry.

As you walked in the front door, the two equally sized bedrooms were to the right. My parents slept in one, and my brothers and I slept in the other. In the winter, Mother covered our beds with layers of quilts because there was no insulation in the house. Some nights we could hardly turn over we had so many covers on us. Mother would put cups of water on our bedside tables, and they would occasionally freeze while we were sleeping. When it rained on our tin roof, it sounded like hail.

UNITED STATES DEPARTMENT OF AGRICULTURE

FARM SECURITY ADMINISTRATION

TENANT PURCHASE DIVISION

REAL ESTATE MORTGAGE FOR ALABAMA

KNOW ALL MEN BY THESE PRESENTS

That whereas the undersigned ....William E. Henderson and Sarah Henderson, his wife................

....

of the County of ......Autauga......., State of Alabama, hereinafter called Mortgagor, has become justly indebted to the United States of America, acting by and through the Secretary of Agriculture, pursuant to the provisions of Title I of the Bankhead-Jones Farm Tenant Act, hereinafter called

Mortgagee, as evidenced by one certain promissory note, dated the ....1st.... day of ....May...., 19..43.., for the principal

sum of ......Three Thousand Eight Hundred and No/100.. Dollars

($ ...3800.00......), with interest at the rate of three per cent (3%) per annum, principal and interest payable and amortized in installments as therein provided, the first installment of ...One Hundred Sixty-four and 39/100....................................... Dollars

($ ...164.39......) being due and collectible on the ....31st.... day of ...December........., 19..43.., the next succeeding thirty-eight installments, annually thereafter, and the fortieth installment, either thirty-nine years thereafter or forty years from the date of said note, whichever date is the earlier; and

WHEREAS, Mortgagor is desirous of securing the prompt payment of said note, and the several installments of principal and interest at maturity, and any extensions or renewals thereof, and any agreements supplementary thereto, and any additional indebtedness accruing to Mortgagee on account of any future advances or expenditures made as hereinafter provided, and the performance of each and every covenant and agreement of Mortgagor herein contained.

NOW THEREFORE, in consideration of the said indebtedness and to secure the prompt payment thereof, as the same matures or becomes due, and of any extensions or renewals thereof, or agreements supplementary thereto, and to secure the performance of each and every covenant and agreement of Mortgagor herein contained, Mortgagor has granted, bargained and sold and does hereby grant, bargain, sell, transfer and convey unto Mortgagee the following described real estate situated in the County of ......Autauga......, State of Alabama, to-wit:

A lot or tract of land, consisting of two parcels in Sections 3 and 4, Township 17 North, Range 16 East, Autauga County, Alabama, in Alabama Farm Tenant Security Project of Farm Security Administration, United States Department of Agriculture, described as follows: PARCEL NO. 1 " Beginning at the Northwest corner of Section 3, Township 17 North, Range 16 East, thence running North 88° 54' 06" East 3957.91 feet, thence due South 1281.71 feet, thence south 88° 54' 05' West 3961.64 feet, thence North 00° 10' 00" East 1281.79 feet to the point of beginning, containing 116.602 acres, more or less." PARCEL NO. 2. "Beginning at the Northwest corner of Section 3, Township 17 North, Range 16 East, thence South 00° 10' 00" West 1281.79 feet to the Southwest corner of the parcel hereinbefore described, thence along the South property line of said parcel North 88° 54' 05" East 455.00 feet to the point of beginning of the parcel hereinafter described, said parcel being 10.00 feet on each side of the following described centerline, South 59° 48' West 214.80 feet, thence South 89° 14' West 145.40 feet, thence South 79° 49' West 436.55 feet to the point of intersection of said centerline with the Northeast right of way line of Alabama State Highway No. 31, the parcel containing 0.366 acres, more or less." Unit No. 14, Alabama Farm Tenant Security, Autauga County, Alabama. The aggregate acreage of the above two parcels being 116.968.

Being the same land that was conveyed to ....Mortgagors.......................................by a certain deed made by

.........Mortgagee........................., dated ......May 1, 1943......, and intended to be recorded simultaneously herewith;

together with all rents and other revenues or incomes therefrom, the rights, easements, hereditaments and appurtenances thereunto belonging and all improvements and personal property now or hereafter attached to or reasonably necessary to the use of the real property herein described, all of which property is sometimes hereinafter designated as "said property";

TO HAVE AND TO HOLD said property unto Mortgagee and its assigns forever.

AND MORTGAGOR, for himself, his heirs, executors, administrators, successors and assigns, does hereby and by these presents covenant and agree:

1. To pay, before the same shall become delinquent, all taxes, assessments, levies, liabilities, obligations and encumbrances of every nature whatsoever which affect said property or the Mortgagee's rights and interests therein under this Mortgage or the indebtedness hereby secured, and promptly to deliver to Mortgagee, without demand, receipts evidencing such payments.

2. Immediately upon the execution of this mortgage to provide, and thereafter continuously to maintain fire insurance policies and such other insurance policies as Mortgagee may then or from time to time require upon the buildings and improvements now situate or hereafter constructed in or upon said Property. Said fire and other insurance policies shall be deposited with the Mortgagee and shall be with companies, in amounts and on terms and conditions approved by Mortgagee.**1A. To pay, on demand, a pro rata portion to be determined by the Government as of the date of the deed to the mortgagor, of any sum paid by the Government (pursuant to Section 2 of the Act of June 29, 1936(49 Stat. 2036) in lieu of taxes under an agreement agreements including the Pro and covering a period including the date of said deed.

William E. Henderson (SEAL)

Sarah Henderson (SEAL)

....
(Mail Address)

....
(Mail Address)

Left, After five years of proving themselves as farmers, Sara and Earl were able to take on a government mortgage for the land and house. *Above top and bottom,* front and side view of Sara and Earl's home.

The bedrooms opened onto a living room that featured a stone fireplace. In the kitchen was a wood-burning stove, which used the same chimney as the fireplace. It was my job to get up first and build the fire. From the kitchen, you could access the screened-in porch, where we did all our canning. We didn't have electricity until I was in elementary school and no phone until I was a junior in high school.

Right outside the screened-in porch was a well house with a manual water pump. I remember being a little guy and trying to work it. I was responsible for priming the pump each day by pouring water in the top cylinder of the pump and pulling the handle down to build the water pressure. Every now and then, the small tank in the pump house would freeze. When we got electricity, the pump operated electrically, and it was much easier.

A short distance from the house stood the smokehouse in which we preserved our meat. We killed, processed, and "smoked" our own hogs, and it worked beautifully. The first really cold day, Papa Henderson and a neighbor would come to help slaughter hogs. We'd drive the hogs into a catch pen, and somebody would hit them on the head with a sledgehammer to knock them unconscious. A hole would be cut behind the Achilles tendon in order to attach a "single tree" yoke (designed to attach a plow to the harness of a mule) so that the hog could be raised upside down by its hind legs using a rope and a pulley. Then we'd cut the jugular and collect the blood because that night for dinner we'd have "blood pudding" and bread. It was my job to keep a fire smoldering to smoke the meat. Once the meat was smoked, we'd put it in the saltbox inside the smokehouse for preservation. We cut the shoulders and the hind legs to make ham. We made chitlins by stewing the intestines after they were thoroughly cleaned. Mother ground some of the meat and made spicy sausage that was delicious.

Beyond the smokehouse was the chicken house, outfitted with about twenty boxes in which our "white leggin" hens could lay their eggs. Most of the time the hens didn't lay the eggs in the house but on the ground in the yard. A rail inside the chicken house allowed the chickens to roost inside at night protected from the coyotes and raccoons. The chickens had free run of the farm during the day and were guarded by our fearless watchdogs. Usually, one rooster could handle about ten hens to make sure the eggs got fertilized. The multi-colored rooster was certainly the "cock of the walk."

For a while, I had a sidekick named Sheila, a half-cocker spaniel trained as a rabbit dog. I had gotten a twenty-gauge shotgun when I was twelve. Sheila would jump a rabbit, and if I didn't shoot it on the jump, she'd bring it back and then I'd kill it. A lot of our meat came from what I killed, mainly squirrels

Top left, Jerry and Ronny in front of the pumphouse, 1945. *Top right,* Earl and Ronny, 1941. *Left,* cousins, from back left: Billy, Mary Jo, Jimmy Dean, Bobby, and Ronny, 1941.

and rabbits. One summer, I was at 4-H camp in Auburn when Daddy found Sheila sucking eggs and shot her. I don't even remember it being a problem for me—it was a rule of the farm. You knew that if you had an egg-sucking dog they were gone. I understood that it had to be done.

Next to the chicken house was the barn with stalls for the animals and a loft to store hay. The barn always smelled of musty hay and sweet manure. We raised "kudzu" hay, a big ole vine that eats up the land and eats you up when you dry rake it and put it up with a pitchfork. Two large cribs were used to store corn. The largest stall could house two mules or horses, and the smaller stall was used to isolate a mare in heat. There were wooden feeding troughs in each stall. A large grazing lot was accessible from the stalls and provided several watering troughs supplied by the well. On the opposite side of the barn was a shed that led to two stalls for the milk cows. A small, adjoining stall was large enough to hold two calves. The birth of animals was a common occurrence.

When I was five, I asked Daddy to teach me how to milk a cow. Well, he didn't want to fool with me when he was getting up before daylight to get a jump on the day and told me, "No." When I heard him get up the next morning, I got dressed and snuck down to the barn after him. As I silently crept up in between the gate and the hay bay, Daddy didn't have any idea there was anyone close to him. And I said, "BOO!" He was holding a brand-new, silver three-gallon milk bucket, a pretty thing; he swung that bucket around, and it cleared my head by a fraction of an inch and hit a post. He tore up that bucket, and then he tore up my rear end! I never scared him again, and he never left me at home again.

Also living in the barn were big gray gopher rats, probably eight inches in length, with long, hairless tails. My brother Jerry and I would go down there at night, and he would shine the flashlight and I'd shoot them with a rifle. It was good entertainment! We had to be careful playing in the barn with our little brother, Tommy. One day, when Tommy was about five years old, he was following Jerry and me through the barn lot and fell in the water trough. He grabbed the edge but his head was still under the water. If we hadn't been there, Tommy probably would have drowned. He had a tight grip on that rim!

Downhill from the main buildings was a two-hole toilet in a tubular structure made of tin where we defecated in the daytime and emptied "slop jars" used during the night. It was almost odorless due to the natural community of organisms depending on this material to live. The only danger in using this

Top, Barn on Sara and Earl's homeplace, built around 1938 by Earl, family, and neighbors. *Bottom left,* Jerry and Ronny, photographed in a studio in downtown Prattville in 1945. *Bottom right,* Sara Ellen Dillard Henderson, 1945.

Above, Tommy, Ronny, and Jerry leaning against pumphouse, 1947. *Right top,* Jerry, Tommy, and Ronny in front of cotton field, 1947. *Right bottom,* Jerry, Tommy, and Ronny in front of homeplace, 1948.

facility was the possibility of wasps building a nest underneath and attacking exposed rear ends. As I got older, I realized I could squat over the hole and almost eliminate this risk.

The "kitchen garden" was about five acres and only about fifty yards from the house. For several weeks, we gathered the produce and prepared the vegetables for canning on our small screened-in porch. For our own use, we canned everything in jars. We used a pressure cooker to seal the quart-size glass Mason jars with lids, and then screwed the tops on tightly. We shelled peas, snapped beans, cut corn off the cob, and peeled tomatoes. We also made pickles from cucumbers in a large ceramic urn, treating them with a brine solution. Our pantry was full of canned goods. Mother made cornbread and biscuits every day, so there was no store-bought bread. For some unknown reason, one year my daddy planted five acres of okra. Willie Mae Frey, my cousin who was six years older than me, lived with us that summer, and we had to pick all that okra. It was not a pleasant experience—sticky, prickly okra is a real pain to pick. But the canned goods, smoked meat, and produce from the garden would carry us through the winter. It was heaven on earth. No doubt we were all much healthier back then.

Every Sunday, my mother would cook "weanie stew" for visitors. She would cut up hot dog weanies and combine them with canned tomatoes and some type of bread in a pot. During that time, friends and family would drop by and then stay for lunch, which back then we called "dinner." They would just let you know they were coming, or Mother would invite them. If they were going to visit in the afternoon, they came after lunch and left before supper. But weanie stew was a big treat for my brothers and me.

For at least five years, we did what was called "truck farming." We produced far more vegetables and produce than we could use ourselves, so we took the extra to market. Five days a week, we would leave home around 3 a.m., the truck already loaded the night before with produce. We would drive to the farmer's market in Montgomery and park in the lot designated for farmers to sell their goods. It was a mosquito-infested area, and we had no insect repellant. I remember sitting in the cab of the truck, hiding from the mosquitos and struggling to stay awake. On returning home, we ate break-fast, and the process started all over again. We went to the field to gather vegetables, reloaded the truck, and got ready for the next 3 a.m. trip.

Occasionally, we would not sell everything and would go peddle the rest of it in the nearby African-American neighborhoods. Race relations, although segregated, were not openly strained at that time. The blacks "knew their place" and we "knew their place." My grandfather was a racist, my father not, me certainly not. Papa Henderson would say, "A nigger is alright as long as he stays in his place." If black people went to my grandfather's house, they had to go to the back door, never to the front door.

Eventually, Daddy developed regular customers of the retail stores in Montgomery; after that, most of our produce was sold wholesale to the retailers. It was a consistent business, much more lucrative than what we had been doing, and very entrepreneurial on my father's part.

My mother and daddy had a loving relationship, and they were together on the parenting. They taught honesty, integrity, and loyalty. In all situations, we were taught to be trustworthy. Daddy had a saying, "Ronny, you don't look good in stripes," referring to the prison garb of the day. Mother was the disciplinarian, but Daddy was the one who meted out the punishment.

I remember when my first cousin, Jimmy Dean Sanford, came to live with us for one summer. All of our cousins loved to come to stay with us in the country. But Daddy's rule was: *If you put your feet under my table, you gonna work.* So they all worked in the fields. Jimmy Dean was four years older than me, and one of those fun-loving, easy-going guys. We were great friends. One day, we were gathering tomatoes to take to market and Jimmy Dean got to throwin' rotten tomatoes at me. I'd pick up a rotten one and throw it back at him. Daddy said, "Stop." Well, we didn't stop. Then Daddy said, "Stop or I'm going to whip both of you." Jimmy Dean didn't believe him and threw one more. Daddy carried us out behind the smokehouse, a belt in hand. Jimmy Dean was almost as large as he was.

Right, Ronny's cousin, Jimmy Dean Sanford, 1944.
Opposite, Ronny's school photograph, 1944.

Daddy started to whip him with the belt, and Jimmy started screaming and running in place. I couldn't help it—I got so tickled. And then Daddy got tickled too and was only able to hit him a couple of licks. Later in life, Jimmy, a motorcycle policeman, was killed in an accident in Montgomery. A guy ran him over at a red light. There is a picture of my cousin in the offices of the Montgomery Police Department honoring his sacrifice.

A FARM BOY BEGINS HIS EDUCATION

Mother was completely devoted to the needs of her family, particularly the success of her children. Even though she had to quit school in the tenth grade to go to work, she was a lifelong, self-taught student. If we used incorrect grammar, spoken or written, she would challenge us immediately. In her mind, education was priority one—my brothers and I knew from an early age that we would go to college despite the fact that there had never been a college graduate on either side of the family. Her greatest pride was, as she phrased it, "my three sons." In her presence, others better not say anything denigrating about any of us or she would give them hell. Right then!

As I got older and started school, my life really changed. When I was in the first grade, my mother asked my twelve-year-old cousin, Willie Mae Frey, to live with us for the school year. We had to walk about a mile through the woods to catch the school bus, and Mother didn't want me walking by myself. Willie Mae was also helpful in keeping the bullies from bothering me while I was on the bus. After that first year, the school bus dropped me off on Highway 31 at what is now called Henderson Lane. Mother knew I was different, a little bit smarter than most boys in our town. She said, "Ronny, don't ever think that you're any better than anybody else. You're just the same as anybody." Then she'd add, "But I don't want you to be a dirt farmer, like your Daddy," right there in front of him. It had to hurt.

School Days
19   44

But that was a happy time for our family. My parents taught teamwork and expected everyone to contribute. I would come in from school, put on my work clothes, and head to the field to pick cotton. On the way, I would grab a biscuit off the stove and pull a radish or onion out of the garden and eat them on the way to the field. Daddy and Mother, and later on Jerry, were already in the field and would be glad to see me. We usually had about twelve acres in cotton. At that time, we didn't have a cottonseed "dropper" to plant the cotton. Our cottonseed sower just spread the seeds, so you'd end up with more plants than you needed. So you had to "chop it" using a six-inch-wide hoe to leave only two or three plants. Using a stroke technique, you'd cut down the extras and pull the dirt back over them. You also hoed to get rid of the grass around the plants. After we had hoed most of the grass out, we "layed the cotton by," which meant running a team of mules pulling a plow that threw dirt on the edge of the cotton to cover any grass that was left. And you didn't touch it again until harvest time.

Top left, Ronny, Tommy, and Jerry, Bridge Creek, 1950. *Above right,* Ronny, Sara, Marie, and Jerry, Bridge Creek, 1950. *Left,* Earl and Sara, Bridge Creek, 1950. *Opposite,* Ronny on horse in the family's cotton field, 1951.

When the cotton boll fully opened in the fall, we would pick cotton from dawn through dusk. By sewing together twenty-five-pound flour bags, Mother made two sacks for each of us. Strapping a bag left and right across our chests, the bags would drag the ground as we moved between the rows, picking from both sides. For some darn reason—and I'll never figure it out, because I have such good eye-hand coordination—Jerry could always out-pick me. At most, I could pick 250 pounds, but he could pick 275. Just frustrated the heck out of me! But I got used to it. Mother would leave the field a little ahead of us to go get dinner ready. We would go home at dark. After being in the field, Mother would heat up leftovers, usually things she had served for lunch—vegetables, tomatoes, cucumbers, and onions.

On Saturday, Daddy would say, "Once you each pick two hundred pounds of cotton, I'll carry you to town and give you a dime to go to the movie." So we'd get up early, while the dew was still on the cotton, so it would weigh more on the scales in the barn. Once we'd picked enough cotton to make a bale, we would weigh it, put it on a wagon, and carry it to the mill to be ginned. We usually produced about a bale and a half per acre on our twelve acres. While in town, Daddy and Mother would visit friends and buy groceries for the following week on credit at Teal Deason's store.

In later years, we protected the cotton by using DDT poison to kill the insect called the "boll weevil" that had devastated cotton crops in the state in the early 1900s. Using the pesticide almost doubled our harvest. Rain often came in the afternoon, so we'd wait until dusk-dark, after the wind settled, to spray the DDT. I would drive the mule pulling the machine that sprayed the poison over four rows. After spraying in one direction, I would turn around and go back through the mist of chemical to spray another layer—no mask, nothing, didn't think a thing about it. As a second-year college student, I had a cold and went to the Student Health Center. They did a chest X-ray, which showed sarcoidosis, a benign condition that may have been caused by DDT. The doctor reassured me, and it went away completely. As a physician, the funny thing about it was that he told me to come back in six months; he knew if it was cancerous I'd probably be dead by then. In 1972, DDT was banned in the United States when we confirmed it caused cancer.

In the heat of late summer, we would make new fence posts to repair our fence line. Daddy and I would go into the woods and find pine trees about six-to-eight inches in diameter. We'd use a straightened hoe to strip the branches and bark. Then we'd use the crosscut saw to cut the top of the tree off and to cut the tree down and then an axe to cut the limbs off. When I was smaller and Daddy and I used the crosscut saw, he would pull and push me back and forth, and I just held onto the other end, keeping it in the groove. As I got larger, I did my part to actually saw. We'd then cut the posts about seven feet tall and soak them in a tank filled with creosote for a few days to preserve them. Then, using a post-hole digger, we'd plant the posts and string the barbed wire in between. Some of our posts, put up in the late 1940s, were still in place in 1970.

In the early 1950s, we suffered some years of drought. Unless you have irrigation, a farmer raising crops is totally dependent on the weather. Daddy was a very talented weather prognosticator, before that was officially available. He had a feel for how the weather was changing, when it was going to rain and when it wasn't. He was just a really bright guy. If it had been dry for a while and then finally began to rain, Daddy would put on his hat, no poncho, and go outside and get a shovel. His excuse to be outside was to divert the water so it wouldn't cause erosion. He always got soaked, and Mother always fussed at him. He really just wanted to get wet and feel the rain.

One hot summer day, Daddy, Jerry, and I had been cutting hay. At that time, we used a mule-driven hay cutter, raking up the hay by hand and tossing it onto a wagon with a pitchfork. We were resting in the shade when Jerry got to playing with the pitchfork and put it right through his foot.

This was especially problematic because we knew Jerry was a "free-bleeder." When he was two years old, he had cut the skin between his toes on the metal base of an ashtray stand and almost bled out. So Daddy picked Jerry up, steadying the pitchfork in place, and carried him to the house, where we got him in the back of the truck and to the hospital. But the wound wasn't even bleeding because the pressure from the pitchfork, which was still all the way through his foot, was like a stopper. Later, both Jerry and Tommy were diagnosed as hemophiliacs by the first hematologist in the state, a pediatric hematologist, Herschel Bentley, MD. From then on, my brothers were very careful.

When I was fourteen years old, I entered a 4-H Club essay contest, writing in response to the prompt, "What It Means to Be an American." The payoff was a purebred Yorkshire pig from a "pig chain," meaning you would win a pregnant pig and give back two piglets so other 4-H'ers could benefit from the chain. So I sat down at the kitchen table and wrote three heartfelt pages. And I won. I got a Yorkshire female, her first time being bred. She

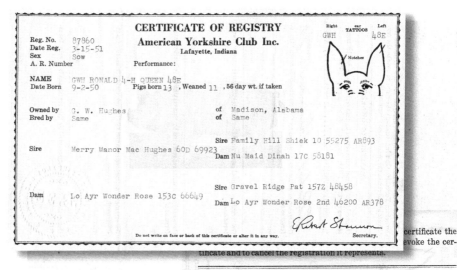

Certificate of Registry for the Yorkshire pig given to Ronny by the 4-H Club for his prize-winning essay, 1951.

had sixteen piglets, but when they were about four weeks old, a virus went through the litter, and they all died except two. We gave those two back to 4-H to continue the chain. We bred the sow again, she had a litter of seventeen this time, and the same thing happened—all died except three. But those three Yorkshire sows survived the virus, grew like crazy, and began spitting out litter after litter. We raised Yorkshire pigs and sold them for years. I got the money, and it was a great experience.

That same year, I also started playing football. The challenge was the twice-a-day practices that began two weeks before school started. Daddy was very supportive of me playing ball, but also needed me to help pick cotton. We negotiated that, during that two-week period, I would leave an hour before morning practice to walk the mile and a half to the high school, and then I'd hitch a ride home to be in the cotton patch by midmorning. I'd pick cotton until the afternoon, and then I'd walk back to the second practice. I was able to get a ride home after each practice with the Boggs family.

I liked playing football because I was in the spotlight. I was reasonably good but wasn't the best one on the team. I played split end, and I could catch the ball. Since we played both ways back then, I played defensive end as well. At that time, the community really rallied around high school football. We had guys, not just dads, who used to come watch us practice. It made you feel like part of the community. As a senior, I had two football scholarship offers, one to Furman University and another to Troy University. I was scouted by Hank Crisp, the one-armed line coach from the University of Alabama. He said, "Son, you're just not quite big enough and not fast enough. So you'll be better off to get an education."

Autauga County High School graduated only fifty-seven students our senior year, but we were more competitive in sports than many larger high schools. The main reason was because of our classmate Robert Hines. He was by far the best athlete on a team—football, basketball, or baseball—but he was just "one of the boys." His exceptional skills as an athlete never went to his head. Robert played right halfback on the football team, just muscle and speed. He was very durable, not easily injured. Robert was built like Mickey Mantle and in baseball had a batting average close to .500. There were only three of us who played all three sports. Robert remains one of my dearest friends.

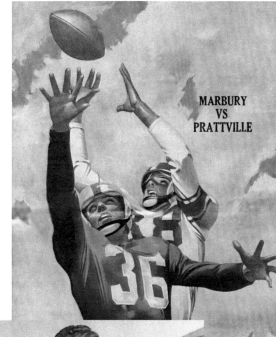

MARBURY
VS
PRATTVILLE

Top left, Ronald sporting missing teeth, knocked out playing football at age 15 years in 1953. *Left,* Ronald, Autauga County High School "Lions" basketball team, 1954. *Above,* Ronald, Autauga County High School "Lions" football team, 1953.

Top left, Ron's lifelong best friend, Joe Allen Chambliss, 1952. *Top right*, "Aunt Gladys" Chambliss, Joe's mother. *Left*, "Big Joe" Chambliss, Joe's father. *Above*, Joe Allen Chambliss, graduation from Autauga County High School, 1955.

Another high school classmate and dear friend, Curtis Mulligan, played quarterback on our team. I would occasionally spend the night at Curtis's house. His father worked in the mills and would come home at 3 a.m. Curtis was a good, kind guy. There are some friends that you don't have a lot in common with but you still love and value them as a friend.

My best lifelong friend, Joe Allen Chambliss, and I have been friends since the age of five. On the football team, Joe played left halfback, and we called him "Crazy Leg Joe." We progressed together academically until, in college, Joe got hepatitis and had a period of disability during which he was home. I didn't go visit because it was a contagious type.

Joe's mother, Gladys Chambliss, was almost related to us by distant marriage, so I called her "Aunt Gladys." She was sort of my second mama, just a dear lady, one of those people who made others feel good. She bragged on me and was interested in my career plans. When I was at their house, Aunt Gladys made me feel a part of the family.

Joe's daddy, "Big Joe," enjoyed the hobby of fighting banty roosters. It was our job, when I spent the night with Joe, to go outside and feed the roosters in their small, separate cages. I remember before one local cockfight, Big Joe told us, "Sons, the Sheriff's Department may be onto us today." It was illegal to bet on the fights. He said, "You boys set on the back row, and if the law comes in, y'all jump out and run up to the highway." They did come in, and we jumped, and we ran. It's exciting to watch, though—you can have a whole arena betting on one rooster, and one gaff through the head and it's over. Big Joe got away with it because the sheriff and deputy sheriff in Autauga County were his cousins.

Big Joe was also the bare-fisted champion in three counties. Men from all over would challenge him, and he would box them using his enormous fists. Recently, I asked Joe, "What influence did your father have on you?" He said, "He gave me courage." Occasionally, the Montgomery high school boys would come over to date our pretty Prattville girls. One night, Joe and I decided to jump them, and that didn't turn out very well. We were a little overconfident.

I met Beth Summerville when she was fifteen years old and I was sixteen. (I am exactly one year and three months older than Beth.) She lived next door to my favorite uncle on my daddy's side, Uncle James. I was visiting Uncle James and his family when Beth came to the vegetable garden to see them. Her brunette hair was shoulder length, and she was very good-looking. About a year later, she invited me on a church hayride, and we began seeing each other regularly.

Beth's daddy, Mr. Calley "Colley" Summerville, didn't trust her older brother with his brand-new car, but he would let me drive it. We'd go to the drive-in movie theater and come back by the Dairy Queen for ice cream. Mr. Summerville ran a barbershop and advertised at the drive-in, so we always had two free tickets. One time, my friend Curtis and his date were going out with us. But we didn't have any tickets for them, so we put them in the trunk of Mr. Summerville's car. They were so heavy that, turning in the parking lot, the bumper got caught on the gutter. We got them out of the trunk, and Beth got behind the steering wheel. Curtis and I lifted the bumper, Beth drove forward, we put them back in the trunk, and drove into the lot. I'm not exactly proud of that escapade, but it was a lot of fun! In the early days of our dating, Beth's parents would go check when the movie was over to make sure we came straight home. My senior year, as co-captain of the football team, one of my perks was to pick a cheerleader for the team, and I chose sophomore Beth. She was eventually made head cheerleader.

Left, Ronald's girlfriend, Beth Summerville, cheerleader for the Autauga County "Lions," 1955. *Opposite top,* George E. Newton, MD. *Opposite bottom left, center, and right:* Sara's "my three sons," Ron, Tommy, and Jerry, 1955.

A GLIMPSE AT A FUTURE

In the tenth grade, I decided I wanted to pursue a career in medicine. My grandmother, Jessie Ora Smith "Mama" Henderson, had developed congestive heart failure and diabetes. I spent a lot of time with Mama Henderson when she was sick. If I wasn't in the field, particularly in the wintertime, I'd ride my bike over to her house and sit and talk to her, get her water or food. She'd tell the world, "Ronny's my favorite grandchild." And she had eighteen grandchildren, so that gave me a boost!

Mama Henderson's physician, Dr. George Newton, would come by to check on her and ask me, "Would you like to go on my rounds with me today?" I'd say, "Yes sir, Dr. Newton, I'd like to go with you." Dr. Newton's philosophy was, "I'm gonna see my patients, examine 'em, and I'm going to give 'em the best medicine." At that time, we didn't even have penicillin, so his arsenal was very limited. He talked to his patients about rest, about exercise, and about taking care of themselves, but that's about all he could do. We'd make a house call or two, and then he'd bring me back.

But Dr. Newton talked to me about medicine and the criteria for becoming a doctor. I didn't have anybody to help me see over the horizon, to see what the future could hold. I couldn't see much further than Prattville at that stage of my life. Dr. Newton was a real mentor who helped me believe I could have a future in medicine. He was also an entrepreneur, developing real estate in Prattville, which is probably where I got my interest in entrepreneurship. He was a valuable asset to me growing up, a true role model.

Overall, my high school education was terrible. The Alabama school systems at that time lacked funding and talented teachers. But my favorite class in high school was physics taught by Ed Riddle, the football line coach. He was an excellent teacher. Coach Riddle ignited an interest in physics and chemistry and provided a more-than-solid foundation in these subjects. I never really excelled in English, math, or history, but I was strong in the sciences.

The last two years of high school I worked at Barnes Grocery store on Friday afternoons and all day Saturdays. The other staff called me "Muscles" because I played football and could easily pick up a hundred-pound bag of feed. I ran the meat counter, where we sold "souse meat," made from the head of a pig, and baloney. I would cut it, weigh it, price it, and then sell it at the cash register. It was a great experience for me. For my work on Friday, Mr. Barnes paid me three dollars. For working all day Saturday, he paid me five dollars. He'd pay me early Saturday morning, and with great pride, I'd immediately deposit that money in the bank. I'd go back to work with that deposit slip tucked in my wallet. And that's when I started saving for college. By the end of my high school experience, I had saved enough money to pay for my first year of living expenses at college without any help from my parents. I am very proud of that, even to this day.

Early on, my daddy had wanted his firstborn son to stay and work on the farm. Mother was adamant that her boys would go to college, and after many heated arguments, she prevailed. Ultimately, both my parents wanted me to go to college but simply couldn't afford to pay for it. Mother had always taught me anything was possible, if you only work hard enough and believe in yourself and your ability to make it happen. As a teenager, I had also read Norman Vincent Peale's 1952 book *The Power of Positive Thinking*, which had a major influence on my thinking. He preached, "If you think you can, you can; if you think you can't, you can't." It's so true.

As the college years for her boys approached, Mother galvanized the family around the singular goal of getting the necessary resources for our educations. When there were no jobs available in Prattville, she got a job at a five-and-dime store in Montgomery and rode the bus back and forth. She would leave very early and come back very late. All the money she earned was saved. Later, she found a job at the Piggly Wiggly in Prattville and rose through the ranks to chief cashier and assistant store manager, receiving numerous company awards along the way. She was always very proud of her accomplishments.

Opposite, Coach Ed Riddle, football line coach and physics teacher at Autauga County High School. *Top,* Jerry with Papa and Mama Henderson in their cotton field, 1953. *Left,* Sara Henderson, Alabama State Checker of the Year, Piggly Wiggly, 1961. *Above,* Earl Henderson, 1953.

As soon as it got around town that I was interested in going to medical school, many of the local businessmen and politicians offered to help find me jobs and scholarships, so I was able to work my way through college. Prattville was a small community of around six thousand people. It was a unique time—I don't think there are many communities in the country now that would take an interest in a country boy like me and open doors like they did. Communities have gotten too big, individuals too self-absorbed to reach out. I'm always looking for opportunities to reach out to young people. I believe that quality attracts quality. A successful person looks around, sees a young person of substance, and reaches out. A young person needs a mentor to help set high goals in areas of interest and then find the resources needed to get there. I've always been fortunate to have caring people around me. I've always made rational decisions, always listened to these mentors. Somehow, I've always felt more mature than other people my age. I never went through the "unruly teenage years" like my classmates.

My maturity may have been, in part, due to an early calling to be a Christian and commit my life to the Lord. As a boy, I was influenced by the genuine spirituality of Mama Henderson, the daughter of a Methodist minister and a devout Christian. Her prayers and daily living taught me to depend on a higher calling. I would go by myself to a special place on our farm—a hardwood thicket where Pine Creek diverges into two smaller streams on the east side of the property—to pray. I went there with a purpose, to work out a situation, to talk things through with God. My belief in God was instrumental in giving me a reason to live and to set a moral course. Having a higher power to call on, to pray and mediate, I probably avoided a lot of pitfalls that could have derailed me. My belief grounded me. At age sixteen, I accepted Jesus Christ as my personal savior at the First Baptist Church in Prattville, Alabama.

Mr. Barnes's brother, Harry, sold insurance from an office in the back of the grocery store where I worked weekends. Harry really wanted me to go to Auburn University. He carried me to Auburn to the ball games and really promoted Auburn. But in talking to numerous people, I decided at the last minute that the University of Alabama would be the more likely path to get into medical school. One of the hardest things I ever had to do was tell Harry I was going to Alabama. At that time, though, you got a better shot at medical school if you went to the University of Alabama. But I had missed regular admissions. Judge James Rice, probate judge in Autauga County and a family friend, made a call to the School of Arts and Sciences at the University of Alabama on my behalf, and Daddy drove me to an interview with the dean. I was granted late admission in the fall of 1955, which was very uncommon in those days.

COMMENCEMENT EXERCISES

AUTAUGA COUNTY HIGH SCHOOL

PRATTVILLE, ALABAMA

1955

Ronald Earl Henderson

Top left, Ronald E. Henderson, graduate of Autauga County High School, class of 1955. *Bottom left,* Ron receiving diploma from Autauga County High School, 1955. *Above,* Calling card.

Ron at home, just prior to entering his freshman year at the University of Alabama.

CHAPTER 2

COLLEGE

UNIVERSITY OF ALABAMA

1955–1958

Mother and Daddy were both excited about me going to college. But Daddy wasn't so sure about me going into medicine and thought that dental school would be a safer bet. He said, "Son, you don't have any contacts in medicine, you don't have anybody to recommend you." And I said, "Daddy, I don't *need* anybody." In fact, the first semester at Alabama he insisted that I enter the pre-dental program; thank goodness the pre-dent program was on the same track as pre-med. It became apparent that most of my classmates were having trouble with the science classes, but I was just *acing* them. So Daddy settled down and was all right.

Although I was doing well in my science classes, it was obvious that I was not wholly prepared for the other subjects due to my inferior high school experience. After testing, I had to take remedial English and math. This was a setback because I had planned to stay in college only long enough to get the one hundred hours necessary to get into medical school. Against the advice of my counselor, I doubled up my efforts. Thanks to Coach Riddle, my high school science teacher, I was able to take physics, biology, and algebra all at the same time. I felt that although I might not be the "sharpest knife in the drawer," no one was going to outwork me. I maintained that philosophy throughout my career, and it's served me well.

This notion of my own intelligence was challenged in my freshman psychology class of three hundred students. In the first week of class, they had us take an IQ test. About a month later, the professor called a female student and me down to the podium in the lecture hall. I had made a 182 on the IQ test. That score means that out of the population of people who have taken that test the scorer is smarter than 99.9%. About 95% of the general population scores between seventy and 130 points. The score of 180 points and above is considered "profoundly gifted." The professor made us both retake the test, and I made 183. I began to think that if I had this God-given gift, I wanted to use it well. It was an incentive for me to work even harder. My commitment to the Lord is, *You have given me this gift, and I'm going to use it.* I'd always thought I was smart, but now I had it documented.

At Alabama, I really hit my stride in the sciences. I just couldn't seem to get enough—I was like a sponge. Organic chemistry and physics were exciting. The physics professor, Eric Rogers, departmental chair, took notice of my success and tried to convince me to go into physics. I had such a good high school background in physics it was a snap for me. I worked hard to memorize the material in history, English, and other subjects. I took English under Dr. Ballinger, a corpulent professor who rode a bike to class. I studied four semesters with him and really enjoyed it, but I got a B each time. But the sciences were always far easier for me.

When I came home for visits, Mother would pack food for me to take back to eat. She was just a nurturing individual. I carried a little brown suitcase with a University of Alabama sticker that Beth had given me for graduation stuck on the side. It was an asset when hitchhiking back to campus. The suitcase couldn't hold much, mostly Mother's canned food. There was a hash house near campus called Sandusky's, and I worked a shift every day so I could have my meals free. They served meats and vegetables, just good, solid food. Mr. Sandusky, a tall, bald-headed guy with a big gut, was very charismatic. Mrs. Sandusky was sort of reserved, an introvert. They were hardworking people who busted their butts, and I was glad to work for them. Not only did I get free food, but I was able to see how they managed the restaurant. I didn't realize it at the time, but looking back I learned a lot from them about how to handle people and manage a business.

Since I wasn't in a fraternity, Sandusky's was my social networking outside of my classes. I met a lot of people there with whom I still keep in touch. Several students from Prattville came to the University of Alabama, some in pre-med. I'd have to go to the library to study because they'd come to visit me in my dorm room so often. Even now, when I see them at our high school reunions, they talk about how hard I worked. But it was intentional because I wanted to get into medical school.

I was two years ahead of Beth in school, so when I went to college, we decided to date other people. But it just didn't work. I dated three or four girls in college, but the chemistry just didn't kick in. Even back then, young women could be so aggressive. Scared the hell out of me! I hadn't had that kind of sex education. Beth and I were just meant for each other.

I was home for Thanksgiving holiday during that first year at college and dropped by to see Mama Henderson. My grandmother and I were tight. As I left, she said, "Be a good boy, son." I was the last person she recognized. When I got back to campus, I had to turn around immediately and come back home for the funeral. Mama Henderson passed away on November 29, 1955. I remember it like it was yesterday. After Mama Henderson passed away, Mother and Daddy brought Papa Henderson to live in our home and be part of our family. He lived there until his death at age 89. In his last few years, Mother cared for him in a loving manner.

The summer after my freshman year in college, a guy named Jack, who drove a Cadillac convertible, recruited me to sell cookware to single working girls for their "hope chests." I borrowed my father's 1956 blue four-door Ford sedan with overdrive to travel to sell the cookware. At the end of six weeks, we had a southeastern sales meeting in Birmingham, and I had sold more cookware than anyone in the region. I was asked to get up and tell the group how I'd done it. I stood up and said, "I don't have any idea, except that I would ask these young women who were working in Montgomery with the Bell Company, teaching school, or working as secretaries to hold parties, and I would make the suggested presentation." I was told to tell them it was for their "hope chests," I assumed "hoping" to get married. I was amazingly successful and made a lot of money that first summer out of college—more than enough to pay my expenses for the second year at Alabama.

When I'd come back to Prattville from college, Mother was oftentimes working at the Piggly Wiggly. So I'd go visit with Aunt Gladys, Joe's mother, at their little Chambliss Texaco Grocery store on Highway 14. She manned the front of the store, so I'd help ring up sales and we'd talk. Aunt Gladys was a lovely lady whom I admired and respected.

Above, Papa and Mama Henderson, 1953.

UNIVERSITY OF ALABAMA
UNIVERSITY, ALABAMA

OFFICE OF THE
PRESIDENT

February 28, 1957

Mr. William E. Henderson
Route 1, Box 31
Prattville, Alabama

Dear Mr. Henderson:

    I congratulate you on the excellent record
of your son, Ronald Earl Henderson. His scholas-
tic achievement qualifies him for the Dean's List
of superior students in the College of Arts and
Sciences for the first semester of the present session.

    To attain this high academic honor requires
both outstanding ability and persistent effort.
We believe that the splendid qualities which his
record indicates will continue to distinguish him
in the remainder of his college career and in all
his later activities.

Sincerely yours,

J. H. Newman
Interim President

Top, second row from top, third from
left, Ron with his HQ 1st Battalion
200th Infantry 31st (Dixie) Division,
Ft. McClellan, 1955. *Bottom,* A letter,
framed, congratulating Sara and
Earl on Ron making the U of A
Dean's List in 1957.

STUDYING AND WORKING MY WAY THROUGH THE UNIVERSITY OF ALABAMA

During my second year in college, I roomed with a fellow student named H.G. McDaniel in the back of a two-story house. We'd walk up a steep set of back stairs and into our rooms. The bathroom was built out over the backyard on stilts, and it was rather cool to take a bath in the wintertime. H.G. studied by the clock, and his good habits rubbed off on me. He'd study fifty minutes, take a ten-minute break, and repeat. He was even more driven than me and eventually became a top-notch endocrinologist.

When I arrived home for the summer after my sophomore year, I carried my solitary brown suitcase into Dr. George Newton's waiting room before even going home. I asked if I could see the doctor after he had seen all of his patients that afternoon. I had barely sat down before I was sitting in front of Dr. Newton's desk. I told him that I did not have a job for the summer and without a job I probably couldn't return to school in the fall. He picked up the phone and asked for Jasper Buckner, who was the super-intendent at Continental Gin Company, one of the two main employers in Prattville. He said to Mr. Buckner, "I have a young man here with me who is making a doctor, and he needs a job for the summer." He received some pushback and said, "I know you can find him a job" and hung up the phone. He told me where to find Mr. Buckner, who kindly introduced me to the director of the "saw room." I worked the 3 to 11 p.m. shift all summer, making circular saws designed to cut the cotton fiber from the seed. I also spent time with Beth as often as possible.

I had joined the National Guard when I was seventeen years old and stayed in for eight years. We received compensation for weeklong camps at Fort McClellan, as well as for required local weekend drills. Colonel Barnes's wife had been my high school typing teacher, and they were both high on me. One weekend, Colonel Barnes had borrowed another colonel's car and said I could use it. After we had drilled in our uniforms, the other guys found out I had use of the car. At that time, Autauga County was dry, and they wanted to go across the county line to get beer. So they all piled in, with their caps off, and we drove to the line and got some beer. For some reason, the MPs were policing Highway 31. They saw the military car, pulled us over, and made us follow them back to the base. I said, "Guys, get straight and get rid of that beer." So they were all throwing beer out the window. The head MP phoned the company commander, who was a really good guy, and asked if I had the right to have the car. He said, "Yes, he does. Sergeant Henderson is the official driver of the car back to Tuscaloosa."

The summer after my junior year, Mr. James McMichael, an old jock, offered me a high-paying summer job at Vandergrift Construction Company. "Mr. Mac" was the shop foreman, so I could work inside the shop any time I could arrange for it. Mr. Vandergrift, the owner, was a big hunter who maintained a flock of pheasants and quail on his farm on the edge of the Alabama River. Part of my responsibility was to feed the pheasants and quail to fatten 'em up. A young black guy, James, helped me out. I noticed James had been slippin' over next door to the house of a prisoner who was out on work release under Mr. Vandergrift's supervision. James was visiting with the prisoner's wife when the husband wasn't at home. I'd tell him, "You don't need to be over there, fella, you're gonna get yourself in *trouble*." The prisoner carried a pistol, and you didn't mess with him. One day, James was over there and all of the sudden the husband's old, dilapidated pickup truck came barreling up the road. James jumped out the screened door, pulling his pants up, and went running and sliding straight down to the river—and we never saw him again! This guy could have killed him if he'd caught him! The prisoner must not have been doing his homework, and his wife was lonely for company.

CHOOSING MY PATH, MOMENTOUS LIFE DECISIONS

As an undergraduate at UA, I had to work very hard taking so many classes, but I was able to apply to medical school after three years. In the last two years as an undergraduate, I made the dean's list all four semesters. Another college pal, Billy Ray Mosley, applied to med school too; he was from Gilbertown, Alabama, and was just a solid citizen. After we applied to med school, we got invited to come interview on the same day. I didn't have a car, so I rode with him from Tuscaloosa to Birmingham. At that time, we didn't get accepted right away but got a letter a few weeks later. Billy Ray and I were both accepted in the fall of 1958, to graduate with the class of 1962.

For some strange reason, I also applied to and interviewed at Tulane University and Emory University medical schools, the high-profile programs in the region. Daddy bought me a new suit for the momentous occasions. I rode the Hummingbird Train to New Orleans; I had never been on a train before in my life. I rode to Atlanta with three other UA classmates who were applying to Emory. We got accepted to Emory on the spot, all four of us. One, Sam Englehart, actually attended. It was crazy for me to even take the time to go. I guess I just wanted to see if I could get in.

Now I had to figure out how to pay for medical school. Mr. Maury McWilliams, Papa Henderson's former partner who owned the Prattville drugstore, introduced me to Dr. G.G. Gill, then the state health officer. Dr. Gill encouraged me to apply for a state scholarship for medical school. There were six scholarship slots and thirty applicants. The scholarship paid $1,250 a year for four years. In return for the scholarship, the recipient would practice medicine for a time in a rural community or repay in cash.

Once I had my professional future in motion, it was time to address my personal life. I was an officer in the ROTC in my last year at Alabama, 1958, and invited Beth up to our formal. On the way, in my father's 1950 Ford sedan with overdrive, I told my Beth that I loved her very much and would like to marry her—if I got the state scholarship. She said "yes" to my proposal, and I soon found out I had been awarded one of the six coveted scholarships. Asking Beth to marry me was one of the most important decisions of my life because she has been an unwavering source of support, comfort, and happiness to me, to all our family, during our fifty-six years of marriage.

At that time, if a guy wanted to marry a girl, it was his responsibility to ask her father for her hand. Mr. Summerville was a lovely man who had reached out to me immediately, just exuding compassion and acceptance. He was about average height with a large head. Like his two brothers, bald at an early age, he had a habit of rubbing his shiny head with his right hand as he talked. As a young man, Mr. Summerville had moved to Birmingham to live with his sister on Twentieth Street while he attended barber school. He moved to Prattville and opened his own shop, eventually the more successful of the two in town. As the most senior barber, his chair was stationed in the back of the shop. He had such a welcoming personality that everybody liked him. Back then, rural people, like my family, came to town on Saturday, so Mr. Summerville would be there until ten o'clock at night cutting hair. He had an outstanding work ethic and a great moral compass.

I went to see Mr. Summerville at their home, and the two of us sat in the den. "Mr. Summerville, I want to marry your daughter," I said. "I love her very much." He said, "Ronald, all I ask is that you take care of her like I have." And that was the end of it. The ritual of me asking for his daughter's hand strengthened the bond between us. He really respected me and I respected him. It was a wonderful relationship.

Beth and I were married on June 28, 1958, in the First Baptist Church of Prattville, Alabama. Following the wedding, her parents hosted a beautiful reception in the garden of their home. We honeymooned at the St. Francis Motel in Montgomery, Alabama. As we checked into the motel, eyebrows were raised because of our youth—I was twenty years old and Beth was nineteen. In those days, as Christians, we waited until our honeymoon before being intimate. The next day, we moved in with her parents and slept in the guest bedroom. When I heard her father cough during the night, I realized that there was no soundproofing insulation in the walls.

That summer I also drove an earthmoving machine, a turnapole, that moved fifteen yards of dirt with each load, putting the base layer on the future airport runway at Dannelly Field in Montgomery, Alabama. Since I was working on the Fourth of July, my base pay of $2.93 an hour was doubled. The week after we were married, Mr. and Mrs. Summerville and Beth brought a picnic out to the worksite for lunch. Mr. Summerville, a member of the Lion's Club, had picked up four barbeque lunch boxes that hit the spot.

Opposite top, Family gathered for Ron and Beth's wedding, 1958. From left: Ron, Beth, Earl and Sara Henderson, Colley and Elizabeth Summerville. *Opposite bottom,* Wedding Party, 1958: Mary Summerville (Tommy's wife), Beth and Ron Henderson, Joe Chambliss.

Top left, The home of Mr. and Mrs. Joe Carr, where Ron and Beth first lived during the medical school years. *Top right,* Beth and Ron on couch, 1958. *Bottom left,* Photograph of Ron in the medical school yearbook, 1958; UAB Archives. *Bottom right,* The Medical and Dental Basic Sciences Building and Dental Clinic, circa late 1950s; UAB Archives.

CHAPTER 3

MEDICAL SCHOOL

UNIVERSITY OF ALABAMA SCHOOL OF MEDICINE BIRMINGHAM, ALABAMA

1958–1962

Beth and I moved to Birmingham in July of 1958, driving a 1954 Chevrolet sedan that was white on top and light green on the bottom, a car we drove all through medical school. We'd bought the car from a classmate, with Daddy generously contributing $270, half the cost of the automobile. Beth paid the other half from money she had made working at Alabama Gas Corporation in Montgomery. We moved into a tiny apartment owned by a Mr. and Mrs. Joseph Carr, seven blocks from the medical school.

When I began medical school, I knew intuitively that this was what God had brought me to life to do. Medical school was a beautiful four-year experience. In the first two years, students absorb huge amounts of subject matter in a lecture setting. Learning medicine was probably the most exciting experience of my life—short of marrying my Beth. I only slept about four hours a night and couldn't get enough of the material read and digested. Beth is fond of saying that she went to sleep with the light in her eyes and woke up with the light in her eyes. That is true, but she slept soundly and never complained. In the third and fourth years, students enter into "clinical rotations," cycling through the specialty areas in the hospital under the guidance of interns, residents, and faculty members. I also started taking calls in the emergency room. That's when I really hit the accelerator—I just loved it.

In the clinical years, we moved to a walk-up apartment on Eighth Avenue right across the street from the medical school. I'd just walk across the street to work. With some hesitation on my part, we purchased a television set on credit so that Beth could have something to do while I studied. We shared the walk-up staircase with cardiologist Cooper Hazelrig and his wife, Jane. At the time we got married, Beth was working for Alabama Gas Company in Montgomery, driving back and forth. She had studied for two years at Massey-Draughn Business School in Montgomery but quit just one week short of graduating to take the job. She was able to get a transfer to Alabama Gas Company in Birmingham, as the assistant to two managers. When Beth got pregnant with our first child, the company put her in the back office because it wasn't "right" to be out front in her delicate condition. She worked at Alabama Gas until our daughter came along in 1961. We had decided that we weren't going to have a child until we could afford it and Beth could be a full-time mother.

Dr. Bill Roberson brought Rhonda Elaine into this world, skillfully handling a breach delivery. He asked me to come into the delivery room, but I didn't want to be a bother because sometimes breach deliveries don't go well. Fortunately, this one did. Once Rhonda arrived, we quickly needed to get out of the small apartment. We bought a little house at 1220 Gladstone Avenue in Crestline that was perfect for us. It had two bedrooms with a bath in the middle, a tiny kitchen, and an open living–dining room area with a picture window on the front. Crestline was full of young families. With my state scholarship of $1,250 a year and savings from Beth's income, we had more than enough resources to meet our needs, as long as we lived rather frugally. And this we did. We bought the house on Gladstone Avenue for less than $10,000 and sold it a few years later for $12,500, making a profit.

In my third year, Dr. Bruce Sullivan, the chairman of the Department of Surgery at the VA Medical Center, recruited me out of the class to do a three-month study that he had designed. Through this project, I was able to meet Dean Jim Pittman, MD, the longest-tenured dean at the University of Alabama. Dean Pittman was also an endocrinologist and provided our study with radioactive iodine. Dr. Sullivan used the radioactive iodine to tag the fat in food fed to post-operative patients so we could calculate the area of absorption by where the iodine was absorbed. Our project was well received and chosen to be presented in Louisville, Kentucky, at the Southern Surgical Conference. Dr. Sullivan asked me to make the presentation, which was really an honor for me.

Opposite left, Dr. Bruce Sullivan, chairman of Department of Surgery, Birmingham VA Medical Center, 1965. *Top left,* Beth and Ron holding newborn Rhonda, 1961. *Top right,* Beth holding baby Rhonda, 1961. *Bottom,* House at 1220 Gladstone Drive, Crestline, Alabama.

I made some really good friends in med school. My classmate and friend Billy Ray Mosley was exceptionally bright and competed with me to be number one in the class. When we'd get back a test, he'd run over to see what I had made, particularly in lab. He went on to establish a successful practice in urology. Bob Henderson was my classmate and friend all four years of medical school. In our fourth year, when we hit the clinics, rumor got out that we were twins. And Bob didn't discount that since I was ranked academically higher than him. He was such a wild card, a risk-taker, that he caught a lot flack from the faculty. One of our physiology professors, Jack Emerson, thought Bob was a communist. Dr. Emerson was strange and bizarre. At the end of med school, Bob went into the military, and we bought his 1954 Volkswagen Beetle, gray in color with maroon interior. Bob eventually established a practice in Rockville, Maryland, as an otolaryngologist.

As a fourth-year student, I had obstetrics as my first rotation. For the remainder of the year, I taught basic obstetrics to my fellow classmates every fourth night and was paid as an acting intern. Dr. Sullivan was a Navy man and tried to recruit me to go into the Navy. We were living on Gladstone when we received an official-looking envelope. I opened it up, and it was an "Honorable Discharge from the US Army." I'd been in the Alabama National Guard for eight years, the required length of my enlistment. I was glad I had served but did not want to be in the US Navy.

When I went to med school and really saw what medicine was all about, I just turned it on. I graduated in the top of my class at number three, but was number one for those who started with me in the class of 1962. We had two students, both named Coleman, who took a one-year fellowship and graduated with our class. Their academic scores were higher than mine; therefore, they graduated number one and number two. Learning medicine was like a hunger. I wanted it all and I wanted it now. If you can have a career that you can look at as a hobby, then you've arrived. And I had that.

At that time, the med school graduated on the campus in Tuscaloosa, and Mother and Daddy both came. Daddy had gotten excited about me becoming a doctor. I've never seen him as happy as that day. He was just beside himself with joy. He'd been so reluctant, so uncertain that I could do it. It gave me quite a boost to see my parents so proud. Those two people were good parents, and they are responsible for the man I am now. While I learned a very strong work ethic from my daddy, I learned to dream and to foster "possibility thinking" from my mother. They were both so happy for me. My aunt Rea, my daddy's youngest brother's wife, had said, "Little Ronny has made a doctor." She thought I had hung the moon and had already given me "the big head," as we say in Autauga County.

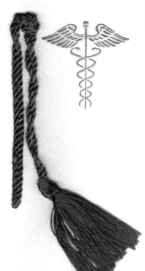

RONALD EARL HENDERSON, M. D.

Top left, Photograph of Ron in the medical school yearbook, 1962; UAB Archives. *Top right,* Program and calling card. *Bottom left,* Ron graduated first in his class of those entering in 1958. From left: two medical fellows, Ralph Coleman and Neil Coleman, Ron, Billy Ray Mosley and Don Curry, UA, Tuscaloosa, Alabama, 1962. *Bottom right,* Ron at graduation from medical school on Tuscaloosa campus of the UA, 1962.

INTERNSHIP YEAR, 1962–63

The summer before I started my internship, when I was a senior medical student, I was hired by Bill Fredrickson, a doctor in Eutaw, Alabama, to take over his practice for a month while he took some time off. Since I didn't have a license to practice medicine, it wasn't exactly legal, but neither was it frowned on in the medical community. Dr. Fredrickson had been the top man in his med school class, but he stuttered so badly that it held him back. But he was an excellent physician.

In his Eutaw clinic, Dr. Fredrickson had a back room with a curtain and a cot. He would have patients in labor come in, mainly African American women, and he would deliver the baby, make sure mother and baby were all right, then send them home. So I took care of his patients. I didn't have a license to practice yet, but I felt confident that I knew what I was doing. Another doctor in town could have advised me if I had needed it. In hindsight, the illegality of it was scary, but nobody paid attention to it back then. It didn't register as *wrong* that I was using his prescription pad and his instruments.

Beth and I stayed in Dr. Fredrickson's home for the month. He and his wife, Ann, coordinated three shifts of servants; it was like the old South. The first shift came in at five o'clock in the morning to fix breakfast and left at eleven before lunch. Then the second shift came in at eleven o'clock to prepare lunch and left about four o'clock. The third shift prepared dinner and were there when we went to bed to shut down the house. It was like slave times, and I bet they paid them next to nothing. It was a strange environment for us, but a unique opportunity.

Top, Mr. Summerville giving Rhonda her first haircut in his barbershop, 1962. *Bottom,* Ron, Beth, and Rhonda at the home of Mr. and Mrs. Summerville on Fifth Street, Prattville, Alabama, Easter, 1962.

Once back at UAB, I chose to do a rotating internship. I took four months of pediatrics (two months in the pediatric ICU and two months on the pediatric wards), two months in the ER (which I loved), and six months of internal medicine at the VA Medical Center treating veterans, which was a great experience. Dr. William "Bill" Dodson was my first-year resident when I was an intern at the VA Hospital. We became good friends during that experience and have maintained a close relationship ever since. Bill went on to become an outstanding rheumatologist.

I had a heck of an internship. In those years, the emergency room staff saw firsthand the racial strife of the Civil Rights era. The policemen and the blacks would come in with gunshot wounds and knife cuts. We treated everybody just the same. Back then, as an intern, I was allowed to perform advanced procedures such as inserting trache tubes and lumbar punctures. The real privilege was having Dr. Tinsley Harrison as my attending physician for two months as a senior student and two months as an intern. Dr. Harrison wrote the textbook *Harrison's Principles of Internal Medicine*, which is still one of the most widely read and regarded textbooks in medicine. This diverse internship prepared me for the practice of medicine as a generalist.

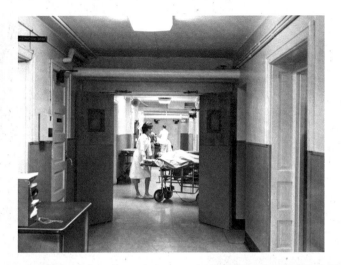

Opposite left, Dr. William "Bill" Dodson, Ron's first-year resident while an intern at the VA Medical Center, 1968; UAB Archives. *Opposite right,* Ron Henderson (center) and Sam Englehardt receive awards from Hospital Administrator Matthew McNulty. Englehardt received "Best Teaching Intern" and Henderson the "Best All Around Intern," 1963; UAB Archives. *Top left,* University Hospital Emergency Room, 1964; UAB Archives. *Top right,* Dr. Tinsley R. Harrison, circa 1964. *Bottom,* University Hospital Emergency Clinic, 1966; UAB Archives.

Top, The house the city of Gordo built for the doctor, which Ron and Beth rented for their stay in Gordo, 1963–1965. *Bottom,* Friends and neighbors, the Housel family: Tenza, Sonny, Paul (center), and Mark.

CHAPTER 4

GENERAL PRACTICE
GORDO, ALABAMA
1963–1965

To fulfill the requirements of the state medical school scholarship, I felt that I should actually practice in a rural area. I researched the opportunities and found that the rural town of Gordo was close to the university. Beth's daddy had grown up in nearby Carrollton, the county seat of Pickens County, so we knew the area. Harold Davis, the Gordo pharmacist, was the head recruiter. The city had built an eighteen-hundred-square-foot, fully equipped clinic with a small emergency room and an X-ray machine. It was a perfect setup that really sold me on going to Gordo. The clinic was right next to the drugstore. In fact, we had a sliding window through which I could "holler" at Harold to order prescriptions. That worked well for both of us, particularly him. All the prescriptions I wrote were filled at Glass Davis Drugs. It was a beautiful relationship.

The community had also persuaded contractors, brothers Ralph and Dave Housel, to build a three-room, one-bath house with a one-car carport for the doctor. We rented this house for our time in Gordo. L.D. "Sonny" Housel Jr. and his wife, Tenza, lived directly across the street from us, and we quickly became friends. Sonny was a charismatic guy who loved everyone. With a great sense of humor, he was just fun to be around. As a companion and a friend, Sonny even made house calls with me. We didn't have GPS back then, so anytime I ventured out into the county in my VW, he went with me as navigator. Sonny's father, L.D. Housel Sr., was a mover and shaker in Pickens County and owned four hardware stores. And then one day, K-Mart and Walmart came to the area and put them out of business. Sonny was just born at the wrong time.

Even with all his hardships, Sonny was just delightful to be around, always cutting up, very current with his knowledge. He transitioned into the construction business and kept on plugging, never complaining. Sonny and Tenza had a wonderful marriage and two sons who have done well. Tenza was always a beautiful woman. As a nurse, she used to come through the hospital dining room in that crisp white uniform, and all the guys would discreetly admire her.

One evening, the Housels had Beth and me over for dinner to grill steaks. Two cars pulled into their driveway looking for the doctor. The driver said that one of the men had a laceration and wanted to be examined. Sonny went with me to the clinic, and when the man walked into the emergency room, we saw no blood. Sonny said, "I thought you were cut?" The man pulled down his trousers to reveal a large laceration on his left buttock. Sonny asked him, "How did you get cut without cutting your jeans?" We both knew the answer. I put eight stitches in the laceration and gave him a tetanus shot. At that time, I was charging $2 per stitch and $2 for the tetanus shot. The man pulled a $20 bill out of his pocket to pay for my services, and I told him my bill was $18. That started a mad scramble among the entire group to find change for the $20. Back at their house, over steaks, Sonny said, "Chief, you may be a good doctor, but you are a very poor businessman. That guy pulled a $20 bill out of his pocket, so you knew he had at least $20. You could've said $28, or $30, or $22, and saved us from having to find change."

That first year, in 1963, our daughter Ellen Elizabeth was born. I did not want to deliver my own child, particularly without any expert help. When Beth went into labor, I was in a panic to get her to Tuscaloosa, where her obstetrician, Dr. Bill Carlisle, practiced. After a few minutes on Highway 82, the Highway Patrol stopped me. When they realized what was happening, they said, "Oh, Dr. Henderson, let us lead the way!" We were very grateful to have an escort to get Beth to Druid City Hospital. The birth was a beautiful experience, and we welcomed Ellen into our family. I remember Beth distracting three-year old Rhonda so I could hold newborn Ellen.

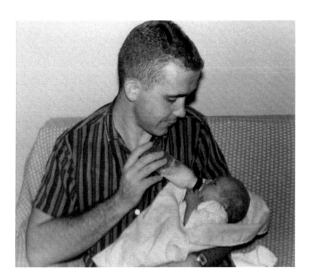

Top, Beth bringing Ellen home from the hospital, 1963. *Bottom left,* Ron feeding newborn Ellen, 1963. *Bottom right,* Ron holding newborn Ellen and two-year-old Rhonda, 1963.

In that little clinic, I had everything I needed, including staff. My nurse, Mrs. Eunice Zeana, was about 5'11" and a lovely Christian woman. Mrs. Opal Elmore was my receptionist. Billy Ray Richardson was my tech, manning the lab and the X-ray machine. I saw thirty-five patients the first day and was soon treating sixty-plus patients a day. There is no way in the world you can really do that many patients justice, but I'd take a history, examine them, treat them, and give them a prescription or refer them on to a doctor in Tuscaloosa. Really, the record keeping at that time was scant. On Thursday, I'd see twenty-five to thirty patients in the morning but take the afternoon off. Beth and I had a little old sixteen-foot speedboat called *The Queen* that we'd take to Pate's Lake to go skiing. We had a great time.

I drove my VW bug all over Pickens County, performing rounds at the hospital and making house calls. The North Pickens Hospital was seven miles west, and I'd make rounds twice a day. At that time, Gordo was a community of about eighteen hundred citizens, with a trading area of about six thousand people. Most of the time, Mrs. Zeana would accompany me on the house calls. She was a large woman, so when we'd get in the bug it would shift a bit. She had a son and a daughter; her daughter still calls me for medical advice. Mrs. Zeana was just a beautiful lady and so devoted to me. Didn't anyone say anything bad about me in front of her. She would whop them!

A local man who had come home to practice medicine in Gordo had moved to Northport and began criticizing the care at North Pickens County Hospital, where I hospitalized my patients. This presented a real challenge. One day, I was called to the weekly stockyard sale to see about a man who had fainted. A farmer named Jim Roberts was in atrial fibrillation, abnormal heart rhythm, and needed to be hospitalized. When I told him I used the North Pickens Hospital, standing his full 6'4", he refused to go. I said, "Mr. Roberts, that is your decision, but I am going to call the hospital and give admission orders, and I expect you to show up. Furthermore, if you don't show up, I will not be available to you ever again for an emergency." I went back to the office, and later that day, the hospital nurse called and gave me the vital signs for Mr. Roberts. I spent that night in the hospital as I converted him to normal sinus rhythm using the drug digitalis. This experience began a beautiful friendship that lasted until the day Mr. Roberts died. He was very demonstrative at a testimonial dinner that the community gave me when I chose to leave Gordo. He also showed up in my waiting room on Tenth Avenue in Birmingham once I had my own ob-gyn practice. It was a wonderful reuniting of great friends.

Above top, The Gordo Medical Clinic, built and equipped by the city of Gordo, 1965. *Above center,* Ron's nurse at the Gordo Clinic, Mrs. Eunice Zeana. *Above bottom,* Ron's receptionist, Mrs. Opal Elmore.

Above top, Ron's first office, Gordo Medical Clinic, 1965. *Above center,* Beth, Ellen, Rhonda, and Ron on *The Queen* at Pate's Lake, 1965. *Above bottom,* Ellen, Beth, and Rhonda enjoy a picnic at Pate's Lake, 1964.

Top left, Sara watching as Ellen and Rhonda cool off in a tin bucket at Earl and Sara's homeplace, 1964. *Top right:* Rhonda, Ron, Beth, and Ellen at the homeplace, 1964. *Bottom:* Earl, Sara, and Papa Henderson at the homeplace, 1964. *Opposite left and right:* Rhonda, Ellen, Beth, and Ron walking a sandy road in Gordo, 1964.

In Gordo, I got to see the full spectrum of medicine, from fractures to traumas. One day, the local piano teacher broke her radius, a bone in the forearm. If you don't set it just right, a thing called Colles' fracture occurs that limits the patient's mobility. I got her X-ray back and said, "Listen, I think you should go to the orthopedists in Tuscaloosa." She said, "No, sir, I want you to take care of me." I had a little handbook about fractures to guide me, and I set it the best I could. I was very relieved when she got back full function of her arm. I was also called to attend wrecks on the highway. It was challenging but invaluable experience. As I did throughout my career, I probably worked too many hours to raise children, but Beth always covered for me. I was there when I needed to be. I was up and down all night with patients, and she was up and down all night with babies!

We also enjoyed a very intimate relationship with the Gordo community. We'd wake up in the morning and there'd be a gift of freshly picked vegetables on our back porch. They just covered us up with love. One night, after the factory shifts in Tuscaloosa changed at 11 p.m., we heard someone in our house. We didn't even think to lock the doors back then. Suddenly, this local guy comes weaving down our hall, vomiting blood. Beth ran to get one of her boiler bowls for him to vomit in, which she later threw away. That was a little too intimate!

But the years in Gordo, without a doubt, cast the mold for the physician that I became. The community of Gordo made it clear that they wanted us to stay beyond two years. It was tempting because it was a good setup and we had made many good friends. But Beth said, "Now wait a minute, if you stay another year, you're not going to be able to leave." She knew I had always wanted to specialize, and it was her recognition of this that was the determining factor in our leaving. In hindsight, the experience awaiting us in Birmingham proved a richer, more expansive one than we could have had in Gordo and, in that, she was right.

Top, Ron, Ellen, Rhonda, and Beth at the homeplace, 1965.
Bottom, House on Queensview Road, Vestavia, Alabama, 1965.

CHAPTER 5

RESIDENCY YEARS

UNIVERSITY OF ALABAMA
SCHOOL OF MEDICINE
BIRMINGHAM, ALABAMA

1965–1968

My general practice experience in Gordo revealed my desire for a specialty. I had really enjoyed longitudinal care, seeing the same patients over an extended period of time. I loved getting to know the patients and their families on a physical, emotional, and spiritual basis. And I also found that I was attracted to general surgery. The practice of obstetrics and gynecology gave me the opportunity to do both. I loved obstetrics, and I loved to operate. I quickly decided that was what I was going to do. I may not have realized these preferences if I hadn't gone into general practice first. It turned out perfectly because when you deliver the baby, the mother becomes your patient for life because she feels like you've done something miraculous. It was an easy decision and one that suited me well.

When I decided to apply for a "residency" or specialty training in ob-gyn early in 1964, I knew this particular residency was very hard to get. There were only three positions available and fourteen impressive applicants. Beth said, "If you want to do ob-gyn, you better go see Dr. Jones." Dr. W. Nicholson "Nick" Jones was the founding director of the UAB Department of Obstetrics and Gynecology, and I had gotten to know him as an intern. I called him to make an appointment, took a half a day off, and drove up there. A great friend of mine, Dr. Sam Englehart, whose father was the director of the Department of Transportation in Alabama, was also interested in a position. His father called Dr. Jones to request a position for Sam, and Dr. Jones told him that he did not have a place for his son although Sam was a very capable candidate. Dr. Jones was not amenable to political pressure.

Jim Alford, who had waited a year to get the residency, Lewis Payne, and I were awarded the three first-year residencies in 1965, to finish in 1968. I believe my educational achievements and my experience in Gordo were the main reasons I got one of the three slots. The three years of residency was a great experience for me. With my Gordo experience, combined with my rotating internship, I had developed an extensive internal medicine knowledge base and taught the third- and fourth-year students not only ob-gyn but also internal medicine. Coming off the farm and having that experience was just God doing great things, opening up one door after another.

For the first year of our residency, each resident was paid a pitiful $200 a month. As the residents progressed, their pay was increased by fifty dollars: second years earned $250, third years earned $300. Yes, they were giving us free food and free uniforms, but it wasn't enough to even pay our bills. With all that training, we weren't making any money. Then Dr. John W. Kirklin came from Mayo Clinic in Rochester, Minnesota, to serve as chair of the Department of Surgery at UAB School of Medicine. In my second year, after I was voted intern resident council president, I went to see him. Dr. Kirklin welcomed me into his office like I was a colleague, not a resident. He listened to me. If you're a leader, you've got to listen, you can't do all the talking. I said, "Dr. Kirklin, this is just not fair. We can't survive on $200 a month." In about three months, he restructured the whole system, paying first-year residents an annual salary of $18,500, a living wage. It was a savvy recruiting tool and it was justified. Dr. Kirklin was—as I always strived to be, based on his example—accessible and receptive. He listened and he acted without hesitation, taking care of his residents. And he expected excellence. At the culmination of my second year, I received the Best Resident Award for the whole university.

Years later, I was bush hogging on the backside of the homeplace farm when Beth came driving up with our children loaded in our van. She said, "Dr. Kirklin wants to talk to you." I said, "Hell, the residents must have struck or something…" I rushed back to the house to call him, and he said, "Ron, I have a new professor coming in, and his wife needs a gynecologist." And I said, "All right, send her to Dr. Bill Roberson." Dr. Kirklin taught me that if you want to talk to somebody today, you move hell and half acres to get to them. You just keep searching until you find them. After I started

Top left, Dr. W. Nicholson Jones, founding director of the UAB Department of Obstetrics and Gynecology, 1967; UAB Archives. *Top right,* Ron and fellow residents at UAB Medical School, 1965. Ron was chief resident his third year. *Bottom left,* Dr. John W. Kirklin, chair of the Department of Surgery at UAB School of Medicine, 1966; UAB Archives. *Bottom right,* University Hospital House Staff Council with president Ronald Henderson, front row, far right, 1967; UAB Archives.

practice, Dr. Kirklin began sending me all of his gyn patients. Just a fantastic guy. As chair, he helped build the UAB hospital system into a leader in the health-care industry, and UAB named its Kirklin Clinic in his honor. Dr. Kirklin had a massive influence on my life.

The two years in Gordo offset two years of the medical school scholarship requirement, and we paid the balance of $2,500 in cash. In Gordo, I had earned $125,000 the first year and $175,000 the second year. At that time, the tax rate was something like ninety percent if you were in the upper echelon, and you hit that bracket when you reached $90,000. So in Gordo, when I made house calls, I'd hand over the cash to Beth, and she'd put it in a coffee can. Back in Birmingham, I said, "We don't want to get caught with this under-the-table cash, they'll put us in jail." So Beth started using the money bit by bit, paying for stuff here and there. In a checkout line, one cashier sniffed the money and said, "This smells like old, musty money." So Beth hung it all on a clothesline to air it out. She probably had $3,000 in that coffee can—*old, musty* money.

Our son, William Eric "Bill" Henderson, was born in Birmingham in June of 1966, during my residency, and was also delivered by Dr. Bill Robertson. This time, I did go in with Beth and it was a slick delivery. I'd told the Lord, *Lord, I will love whichever you decide to send me, but if you see fit, I'd like to have a boy.* It was a beautiful delivery. We had planned to have six children, but once we had two girls and a boy, we decided that our family was complete.

Top left, Beth in hospital with newborn Bill, 1967. *Top right,* Ron and Bill, during four-month rotation in Mobile, Alabama, Easter, 1967. *Bottom,* Rhonda, Ron, Bill, and Ellen at Sara and Earl's home, Easter, 1967.

DRS. WALDROP, ROBERTSON, GRAY & HENDERSON

2700-10th AVENUE, SOUTH

BIRMINGHAM, ALABAMA 35205

EDWIN G. WALDROP, M.D.
WM. H. ROBERTSON, M.D.
GENE W. GRAY, M.D.
RONALD E. HENDERSON, M.D.

PRACTICE LIMITED TO
OBSTETRICS, GYNECOLOGY
AND STERILITY
TELEPHONE 328-5570

EDWIN G. WALDROP, M. D.
WILLIAM H. ROBERTSON, M. D.
GENE W. GRAY, M. D.

ANNOUNCE THE ASSOCIATION OF

RONALD E. HENDERSON, M. D.

FOR THE PRACTICE OF

OBSTETRICS AND GYNECOLOGY

AT

2700 10TH AVENUE SOUTH
BIRMINGHAM, ALABAMA

HOURS BY APPOINTMENT   TELEPHONE: 328-5570

EDWIN G. WALDROP, M.D.	W. H. ROBERTSON, M.D.	GENE W. GRAY, M.D.	RONALD E. HENDERSON, M.D.
Reg. No. 3375	Reg. No. 5115	Reg. No. 1183	Reg. No. 995
Res. Phone 879-4402	Res. Phone 323-1376	Res. Phone 967-0904	Res. Phone 822-7960
2700 - 10th AVENUE, SOUTH		OFFICE PHONE 328-5570	BIRMINGHAM, ALA. 35205

For.. Date............................

Address...

℞

This RX May NOT be Refilled ☐
This RX May be Refilled At ☐
Intervals Indicated ....M.D.

SCHEDULE OF OBSTETRICAL FEES

The charge for prenatal care of the mother, delivery of the baby and
6 weeks check up for the mother 230.0
Laboratory 10.0
Anesthesia (if administered by doctor) 20.0
Circumcision (if done) 15.0

WHAT IS INCLUDED:

1. Physical examination

2. Prenatal care

3. Delivery and care of the mother in the hospital

4. Post partum check up for the mother at 6 weeks and 3 months after delivery

5. Laboratory: Charge shown above, includes routine urinalysis each visit;
   Hemoglobin determinations; Serology; blood typing and Rh determination
   (if negative – titre tests are an additional 6.00 each)

6. Anesthesia: If administered by hospital anesthetist they bill you
   separately; if administered by one of us - 20.00, as shown above;
   however, there is an additional charge in either case by the hospital
   for use of the anesthetic equipment.

WHAT IS NOT INCLUDED:

1. Surgery for the mother (Cesarean section - 200.00)

2. X-rays (not necessary in most cases)

3. Injection medication

PAYMENT IS DUE IN FULL UPON DELIVERY; HOWEVER, IT IS HELPFUL TO THE PATIENT
TO MAKE PAYMENTS DURING PREGNANCY EVEN IF YOU HAVE INSURANCE, BECAUSE
ALMOST ALL OF THE INSURANCE COMPANIES DO NOT PAY THE DOCTOR BILL IN FULL

Unless requested by the patient, obstetrical statements will not be sent until
after delivery

A WORD TO OUR PATIENTS:

You are now in the fortunate position of having not one but four doctors at your call. We (Drs.
Waldrop, Robertson, Gray and Henderson) alternate night calls so that you will always have the
benefit of a doctor that has not been up two nights in a row. We feel that we can give you the best
care with this arrangement.

Dr. Edwin G. Waldrop   Dr. Wm. H. Robertson   Dr. Gene W. Gray   Dr. Ronald E. Henderson
Office Phone 328-5570   Office Phone 328-5570 Office Phone 328-5570 Office Phone 328-5570
Home Phone 879-4402   Home Phone 323-1376   Home Phone 967-0904   Home Phone 822-7960

IF NO ANSWER, CALL 323-2555

RONALD E. HENDERSON, M. D.
OBSTETRICS AND GYNECOLOGY

HOURS BY APPOINTMENT   2700 10TH AVENUE SOUTH
TELEPHONE: 328-5570   BIRMINGHAM, ALABAMA

CHAPTER 6

PRIVATE PRACTICE
BIRMINGHAM, ALABAMA
1968–1994

After the residency, Beth and I had planned to return to Tuscaloosa to be close to the many friends we'd made while in Gordo. That plan was derailed by an offer we couldn't refuse, from the most respected obstetrical-gynecological practice in Alabama, Waldrop, Robertson, and Gray at St. Vincent's Hospital in Birmingham. After only three months of trial period instead of the usual two years, they offered me full partnership.

Bill Robertson and Ed Waldrop, being senior, each had an office and one treatment room. Gene Gray was working out of a single room as both his treatment room and office. He would stretch out a curtain, step outside the door, and the patient would undress. They had only one staff member, Mrs. Turner, making all the appointments, calling the patients, doing all the administrative stuff. The doctors were dedicated to excellent care and felt strongly that they should be at the bedside of a patient in labor, which left them unable to attend to scheduled appointments. The whole system was totally inefficient.

We had a meeting at the Birmingham Country Club, where I recommended some business changes and improvements to patient care. Gene saw the value, but Ed and Bill, rather than go through the upheaval, chose to give up obstetrics. At the end of my first six months, Dr. Gray and I were left with the patients of a four-doctor obstetrical practice.

We moved our practice to a little place on Tenth Avenue and began a partnership of shared expenses and profits on a fifty-fifty basis. I brought with me the wives of most of the residents and medical students. At that time, the residents and the medical students didn't have medical insurance. So we delivered their babies for free, gladly. For the rest of my career, all those doctors referred their patients to me. If you take care of people, it comes back in spades. After a couple of years, it became apparent that although we were splitting the profits fifty-fifty, I was putting seventy-five percent on the books, plus handling the business side. Gene and I had very different work ethics, and the partnership just didn't work out.

At the end of two years, I chose to begin practice by myself. I moved back into our original office across the street from St. Vincent's Hospital, which allowed me to monitor patients in labor and still see office patients. At that time, I was performing spinal blocks to reduce pain during labor, but I later started using epidurals. I had six rooms including an office, a lab, and four treatment rooms, all blowin' and goin'. The setup continued for eighteen months, and I delivered between forty and fifty babies per month.

When I came to St. Vincent's after my residency in 1968, I received an incredible amount of help and support. The chief of anesthesia, Dr. Alfred Habeeb, was just an amazing individual. He took me under his wing and was so good to me. I was much younger than he was, but within six months of knowing him we were more like equals, advisor and confidant for the other. He was also one of my biggest cheerleaders and a good friend. He opened a lot of doors for me that I wouldn't have had access to as a tenant farmer's son. For one thing, he laid the groundwork for me to become a member of the Birmingham Country Club.

Since Waldrop and Robertson had given up obstetrics, the administration had to choose a departmental chair from the remaining staff. The head Sister at St. Vincent's had asked around, first calling Dr. Robert Barnett, a clinical professor at UAB. He recommended me. Then she called Dr. Nick Jones to address the gynecological component, and he recommended me as well. Six months after my entering practice at St. Vincent's, I was made chairman of the Obstetrics and Gynecological Department. I had no managerial experience besides running my Gordo practice. And I was the new guy on the block.

At that time, the protocol for deliveries was for the nurse to sedate the patient, using scopolamine and Demerol. Scopolamine causes amnesia; the patient has no memory of the delivery. It is healthier for mother and baby to do without these medicines and their side effects in delivery. Although

Top, House on 4301 Kennesaw Drive, Mountain Brook, Alabama, 1970. *Bottom left,* Dr. Alfred "Freddie" Habeeb, Ron's friend and chief of anesthesia at St. Vincent's Hospital, mid-1980s. *Bottom right,* Beth, Ron, Rhonda, Ellen, and Bill, Easter, 1970.

I caught a lot of flack, keeping the mother fully conscious also allowed me to open the delivery room to the fathers. St. Vincent's was the first hospital in the Southeast to welcome fathers into the delivery rooms.

We also changed the common practice of nurses delivering babies when the doctors weren't making it to the hospital in time. I established a rule that if a doctor had a patient in active labor (four centimeters dilated), he or she should be in the hospital. I set up a "call room" where an obstetrician could nap until needed. At that time, we were using saddle blocks, though later we started using epidurals. When I was the obstetrician on call, the nurse would sedate the patient for me based on previous orders. When they needed the block the nurse would call me. I'd get up, deliver the baby, go back to bed, and it wasn't a problem.

When I came on board as a thirty-year-old chief and started trying to change these ingrained practices, I was met with indignant resistance from certain doctors. I had to absolutely threaten their hospital privileges to get them to comply. It was tough; but you know, right is right. It went more smoothly once they realized that I was serious. Among other things, I was called a "change agent," but I just tried to do was what was right for the patient. There is no reason for us to be here if we're not going to take care of the patient.

One Sunday morning a month, I met with the St. Vincent's executive committee, and although I was younger, they considered me a full member. After three years, I was made chief of staff—a rapid rise.

Top left, Beth and Bill, Sara and Earl's home, Christmas, 1969. *Right,* Earl, Ron, Papa Henderson, and Bill. *Bottom left,* Rhonda, Earl, Sara, Bill and Ellen.

THE EARLY YEARS OF PRIVATE PRACTICE

After that first year in practice by myself, I knew doggone well I couldn't see all the patients I had acquired. I realized then that I was going to have to build a practice of more than just me. In 1969, I started trying to recruit Dr. Ernie Moore, the son of a physician from Tallassee, Alabama. Ernie wouldn't commit, so I called him and said, "Ernie, dammit, you've got to get off the pot. I want you to come, but if you're not going to come, you've got to tell me." He said, "I'll be there, Ron." He was waffling because he was tempted to go back to his hometown of Tallassee, where he was moonlighting. So Ernie, who was extremely attractive as a physician because of his confident and caring attitude, came in with me. For the next few years, we practiced together in a harmonious partnership. I was a preventive medicine doctor and would fuss at my patients about losing weight and exercising. But if I fussed at them too much about losing weight, they'd start seeing Dr. Moore, who was more easygoing.

Ernie and I got along well, even through my terrible automobile accident and recovery in 1974. The accident was my own fault. One foggy and rainy night, the hospital called about a patient with placenta previa, an obstetrical condition that can cause the patient to bleed out and die. I told the staff to prep her for surgery. By that time, we were living on Kennesaw Drive in Mountain Brook. I went down to the basement where the cars were kept, and Beth said, "Why don't you go in my car?" She was driving a big ole Lincoln Town Car. I said, "I'll be all right." I should have listened to her; it would have been a nonevent in her car. Wearing my scrubs, I got into my 240Z Datsun. Apparently, I ran a red light at the intersection of Euclid Avenue and Montevallo Road. A Rambler, a four-door, heavy sedan, crashed its

Left, Ron and Ernie, St. Vincent Hospital, third (ob-gyn) floor, circa 1976. *Opposite right,* Ron's medical assistant, Wilma Conner, receiving the Associate of the Month Award at Henderson & Walton in the 1980s.

bumper right into my door and pushed me into a pole. I didn't remember a thing after that because I had about seventy-two hours of amnesia. Later, I saw the ambulance driver, and he said, "Doc, you were real funny, you raised up on both elbows and said, "Listen, slow this damn thing down, we already had one wreck tonight!" The police sent an officer to the house to tell Beth, who thought maybe I had a broken leg or something minor. Beth was able to track down Ernie, who rushed to the hospital to attend to the patient.

The impact crushed my pelvis and fractured the neck of the left femur and two places of that same femur. The diagnosis was a crushed pelvis with a floating fragment, as well as a fracture of the superior and inferior ramus of the pelvis. I was in the ICU for three weeks. I found it remarkable that I had friends coming from all over to visit me—medical students I had taught, fellow residents, patients—it was just amazing. Beth would try to talk to them outside my door, but I would wave them into the ICU. It was just before Christmas, and I got more than three hundred get well and Christmas cards *in one day*. Beth had to carry them home in boxes. Dr. Max Austin, a fellow ob-gyn and friend, brought Beth and the kids a Christmas tree and even put it up for them. On Christmas morning, I had the nurses push my bed down the hall to the nurses' station so I could call to wish my family a Merry Christmas as they opened presents.

I lay on my right side and on my back the entire six weeks I was in the hospital. After five weeks, they moved me to the tilt table so that I wouldn't faint when I tried to stand. It took two days and three tries before I could stand erect. When I was finally discharged from the hospital, I had to move around in a wheelchair for a while, which nearly drove me crazy. I tried to read all those wonderful cards but couldn't because of crying. I slowly progressed from a walker to crutches and was totally obsessed with getting back to work.

At the office, I had a sofa on which I would normally take power naps after noon surgery. After the accident, as I healed, I'd see two patients, slip into the office, and lie down on the sofa. My medical assistant, Wilma Conner, would help me to the sofa, cover me up with a blanket, and let me rest for fifteen minutes. Wilma was a very important person in my life. An African American woman in her early forties, she came to work for me without any medical experience—but she had fantastic people skills. She could absolutely charm the patients. If I were running late for an appointment because of surgery or delivering a baby, Wilma would keep them happy. She did everything for me. After the wreck, she even drove me in my car down to the State Board of Health meetings. She was a powerhouse, working 24/7, never late, always dependable. Wilma is also quite the character, using colorful language, which is always entertaining. Everybody loves Wilma Conner.

For several months following the wreck, Ernie Moore picked up the slack in my patient load, and he was just covered up. Talk about loyalty—friends are friends, but Ernie took calls every night for three and a half months with no complaints. On one weekend only, he got a fellow ob-gyn to cover for him. Other than that, he never took a night off. He just picked it up on his shoulders and carried it, just a great friend. We had patients backed up, waiting out on the front lawn to see Ernie when he could get to them. We lost very few patients.

As my recovery progressed, I turned my attention to the challenge of operating and delivering babies. Nobody could tell me how to get from the scrub sink to the operating table without contaminating the area with my walker. I asked several surgeons, and not one had a single idea. Finally, I was standing at the sink and it dawned on me. I would scrub, they'd hand me a towel, and I would dry my hands. They'd throw a sterile sheet over my walker, which I would use to move into the operating room, and then they would gown and glove me. Then I'd move the walker, still draped with a sterile sheet, to the side of the operating or delivery table. The first patient I operated on after the accident was June Elmore, the daughter of Mrs. Zeana, my nurse in Gordo.

About eighteen months after the accident, I had the eleven-inch steel plate that had been screwed to my fractured femur and hip surgically removed. It had begun to really bother me when the barometric pressure changed. The surgery was not a pretty procedure; the doctor had to make an incision the length of the plate and then disengage the plate from the femur. A few days after the surgery, Wilma Conner drove me to Montgomery to attend a State Committee of Public Health meeting of which I was a member. Wilma and I checked into rooms at my usual hotel. I had brought a few bandages because my wound was seeping a bit. In the middle of the night, I woke up, wet all over with blood. I stood up and thought, *What now?* I showered and put on a fresh bandage to stop the drainage. I wadded up all those bloody sheets, piling them right on the spot where the blood had seeped through to the mattress, and spent the rest of night on the sofa. The next morning, Wilma came to get me and said, "REH, *what* happened here?" I told her and she said, "They're going to think somebody was slaughtered in here!" I never heard a word from the hotel.

Recovering from the accident was a valuable learning experience. At thirty-eight years of age, I'd always thought I was tough, but the accident confirmed it—I came back with a vengeance. I think my response stemmed in large part from the parenting I'd gotten, which reinforced the idea that I could do anything if I set my mind to it. I had gotten myself in a situation where I had to prove it. That insight would prove essential in the challenging times yet to come in my life.

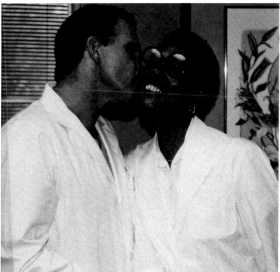

Top left, Ron and Bill, Christmas, 1975. *Top right,* Ron, on crutches from accident, and Ernie, 1975. *Bottom left,* Caricature. *Bottom right,* Ron, showing his appreciation to Wilma, in the 1980s.

SERVING PUBLIC HEALTH IN ALABAMA

Having "manned" the public health clinic every Thursday afternoon in Gordo, I had seen firsthand the tremendous need to improve the health care of the poor in this state. From 1974 through 1981, I was a member of the State Committee of Public Health in Alabama, the body that oversaw indigent care clinics in the state. My first two years, I had a seat by virtue of serving as chairman of the Council of Medical Service. After that, I ran against an incumbent, a Birmingham internist, and earned a five-year stint to address public health.

In the late '70s, the Alabama State Department of Health was driven by a top-down system. I had been in Gordo and knew that the counties, for a lack of a better phrase, "sucked hind tit" because Montgomery made all the decisions on health-care policies. It was evident that we needed a new structure. I visited North Carolina to better understand their successful template of dividing the system into districts. Alabama already had established political districts, which was a perfect setup. Through logic and persuasion, I sold the concept to the rest of the committee. A state health officer would be located in each of the districts to work with the district director, who would ultimately determine policy for the district. Policy issues wouldn't have to be carried to Montgomery. The district system is still in place today, which proves that if you get the right model, it will survive.

As a member of the State Committee of Public Health, I also was on a council to address the issue of unlicensed midwives operating in the state. In Gordo, I had been exposed to the "granny midwives," untrained, usually extroverted females who had taken it upon themselves to assist in home deliveries. Poor women didn't have the transportation and couldn't afford to go to a doctor for delivery. One night, a patient was brought in to me who had been in labor nineteen hours in the care of a "midwife," who had no idea how to handle the situation. I had to do an emergency cesarean section. The Nurse Midwife Act was passed to ensure that anybody calling herself a "midwife" was trained. We certified the trained ones, most of them nurses. The untrained "granny midwives" went out of business because it became illegal for them to deliver babies. Most of the certified midwives ended up working in the major population areas. I was hoping to get them out in the rural areas, but that is not what happened. Gradually, low-income women had more access to transportation and were able to get to the doctors. Once the Medicaid program was enacted and funding was available, obstetricians delivered the insured babies.

Henderson Elected Head Of Medical Association

Prattville native, Ronald E. Henderson, M.D. has been elected President-Elect of the Medical Association of the State of Alabama. He will be installed as President of the Medical Association at the 121st annual session of the professional association to be held next year in Huntsville.

Now in private practice in Birmingham, Dr. Henderson received an undergraduate degree from the University of Alabama in 1958 and a medical degree in 1962 from the Medical College of Alabama.

After completing an internship at the University of Alabama Hospitals and Clinics, he established a general medical practice in the rural Alabama community of Gordo in Pickens County in 1963.

He practiced medicine in Gordo for two years returning to the University of Alabama in 1965 to complete a residency in obstetrics and gynecology. He was named chief resident and instructor at the medical college in 1967.

Dr. Henderson has held numerous hospital and faculty appointments including that of chief of obstetrics and gynecology at St. Vincent's Hospital in Birmingham and clinical assistant professor at the Medical College of Alabama.

He has served in leadership positions as a member of the Medical Association Board of Censors, Board of Medical Examiners, State Committee of Public Health, State Health Planning and Development Agency Board, American Medical Association House of Delegates, Jefferson County Medical Society, and the Executive Committee of St. Vincent's Hospital. He is also active in a number of religious, professional, business and civic organizations and is listed in the Who's Who of the American Medical Association.

The Medical Association of the State of Alabama was founded in 1873 and is the state's largest physician organization.

Henderson Elected To State Post

Ronald E. Henderson, M.D., Birmingham obstetrician-gynecologist and son of Mr. and Mrs. W.E. Henderson of Prattville, has been elected by the Medical Association of the State of Alabama to serve as a member of the State Board of Censors.

The election took place during the April Annual Meeting of the Association in Montgomery and the unanimous vote came from the Association's College of Counsellors and House of Delegates.

Dr. Henderson is married to the former Beth Summerville, daughter of Mr. and Mrs. C.W. Summerville, of Prattville.

He graduated from the University of Alabama School of Medicine in 1962 and practiced in Gordo (Pickens County) from July 1, 1963 to July 1, 1965, at which time he opened his practice in Birmingham.

Top, The Prattville Progress, June 4, 1981.
Bottom, The Prattville Progress, 1976.

As president of the Medical Association for the State of Alabama (MASA) in 1982–83, I believed that doctors needed to be informed of the impending changes concerning the consolidation of the health-care system. All kinds of ideas were being bandied around; hospital administrators were considering hiring doctors directly to save on costs, doctors were considering forming unions. I was reading and keeping abreast of the new information and trying to disseminate the important points to Alabama doctors. So that I could read as much as possible, Beth did the driving as we journeyed all over the state to give a canned speech to audiences of medical professionals. I felt that issues needed to be clarified to fend off an angry, disruptive reaction from the doctors. Also, in the audience of almost every city there would be a doctor who would refer a challenging, complicated gynecological patient to me, netting me a new patient.

Also as president of MASA, I was working to bring optometrists, podiatrists, chiropractors, and other paramedical professionals under the regulation of the State Committee of Public Health. I was approached by journalist Mike Wallace, who was conducting interviews for a segment to run on the CBS television newsmagazine show *60 Minutes*, at that time a program known to be anti-physician. Because they often ambushed interviewees in the parking lot, I borrowed an old Honda from one of the farm workers to drive to Montgomery, leaving my Mercedes at home. I switched my Rolex watch for a Timex, and I was ready for Mike Wallace.

I met Wallace and his crew of about twelve mid-morning on a Saturday in the MASA office suite in Montgomery, where they set up lights and cameras. Wallace had been told that we were trying to bar paramedical people from the state, which was totally false. After about fifteen minutes of questioning, during which time this became apparent, he suddenly stood up and said to his colleagues, "What the f— are we doing here?" They packed up and left. On Monday morning, he called and said, "Dr. Henderson, you will hear nothing further about my visit because I have killed the story. We thank you for your courtesy." It was an interesting encounter.

Opposite left, A book published by the physicians of Henderson & Walton Women's Center, 1992.
Opposite right, Ron treating a nurse in the Henderson & Walton Women's Center, about 1985.

THE FIVE F'S: CARING FOR WOMEN AND FOR LIFE IN GENERAL

Over my years in practice, I developed certain theories about how women may best take care of themselves. As more women enter the workforce and take on professional and financial responsibilities, I've noticed a critical need for maintaining balance in their lives. Although women are considered equals at work, they are still the ones who have the babies and who ultimately take on the larger caretaking role. A woman trying to balance the roles of professional and mother has to work at controlling stress, which includes taking time for herself. I would tell my patients, "You owe it to yourself to take time for yourself. You're a role model for your children, particularly your girls. When you take time for what's in *your* best interests, that's also in your children's best interest—whether it be educating yourself, personal fitness, buying clothes for yourself, just feeling good about yourself, whatever it is."

To maintain the balance in life in general, I'd often refer to the "Five F's" in life: Faith, Family, Friends, Fitness, and Finance. When a person strikes a balance among those aspects of life, maintaining each in a comparable degree, life seems to move along more smoothly. I try to live by the Five F's myself. My faith means everything to my well-being. Finance is important, but that shouldn't be your driver. I believe that you've got to have the faith to make all the rest work. The five F's equal "Fun" if properly balanced. Actually, it's a good philosophy for men and women alike.

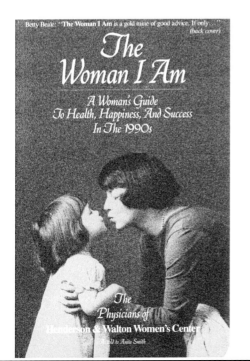

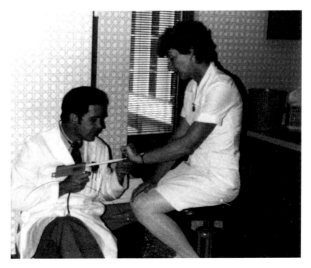

Top left, Rhonda riding Go Boy, Ellen riding Big John, and Bill riding Socks,1972. *Bottom left,* The "new herd" acquired as part of land purchase, 1971. *Top right,* The valley on the new farm, 1972. *Bottom right,* The trailer was brought to Twin Valley Farms in 1972.

CHAPTER 7

TWIN VALLEY FARMS, LLC
PRATTVILLE, ALABAMA
1971–PRESENT

Because of our strong family ties and love for Prattville, we made the trip home every weekend that I wasn't on call. I would help Daddy with his small herd of cows and do what I could to help maintain the farm. Our time was split between the Henderson and the Summerville families. In early 1970, my father-in-law urged me to look at a beautiful piece of property off of US Highway 14, west of Prattville, on County Road 41. He used to quail hunt on the property and had heard, through a customer in his barbershop, that it was going to be put up for sale. As we made the approach from County Road 41 and the stunning contour of the farm unfolded before me, I knew I had to have the land if I could afford to pay for it.

The land was part of the old Paul Smith plantation that had once covered three thousand acres. At that time, the parcel we were looking at was owned by Dr. Henry Ward, a professor at Huntington College in Montgomery. Dr. Ward's ancestors had left the land in a trust with the First National Bank of Birmingham, now AmSouth. I established a relationship with the trust officer for the bank, and rather quickly, we had signed a letter of intent to buy the property. Because Dr. Ward and his wife were still living in the main house on the property, we carved out fifteen acres around their homeplace to be bought at the time of their death. At their passing, we held 865 acres of what is now Twin Valley Farms, LLC. Over the next few years, we were able to add four hundred acres that we bought from the state through an open bid process. Another four hundred acres to the east of the original land came up for sale, and we quickly arranged to purchase that piece of property as well. Now the farm encompasses approximately sixteen hundred contiguous acres. I have made an offer on four hundred acres southwest of the property and am still in pursuit of consummating that deal.

We took possession of Twin Valley in January of 1971, and the next year, we pulled a singlewide trailer into a pasture so that our family could stay on our own land before we built the house. In slave times, the landowner had tiered the land to plant, so we had a nine-foot hill with levels circling around it. With a bulldozer, I flattened the top of the hill, disked it, and sowed centipede and Bermuda grass seed to ready it for the trailer. As part of the purchase price of the original land, we got some 125 cows and a few calves in the deal. We had been running cattle on my family's homeplace off of Highway 31, north of Prattville, and we combined the two farms as one operating entity, bringing our total population of commercial grade cows to around 155. Our friend from Gordo, Sonny Housel, built our first barn at Twin Valley Farms.

The original name of our farm was "REB Ranch," combining the initials of our children's first names. Growing up, the children remember Fridays as days spent anticipating the trip "home" to Prattville. We were all filled with excitement going and had tears in our eyes when we left. Weekends were family times—good times when I was around all day, even if that meant driving a tractor or building a fence somewhere. Weekends were also a time with grandparents and relatives, something a lot of children never experience. I would carry my "little black bag" and take blood pressure and offer advice to family.

We got to know our neighbors at the new farm, the well-respected Wadsworth family. As young men, the three brothers, Leonard, Jack, and Ed Wadsworth, had begun farming their 1,900 acres close to the Alabama River. Leonard managed the timber, Jack farmed the row crop, and Ed raised the cattle. The brothers lived together in the same farmhouse and worked out of the same checking account. Eventually, they raised their families in that same farmhouse. The brothers became very successful and continued to divide up the profits. They were community-oriented and served on many committees for the town. Ed's wife, Hope, owned the dress shop downtown across from Mr. Summerville's barbershop. The Wadsworths are just good folks.

Ed was in his late sixties when we met, and quickly became my mentor in the cattle business. He drove a little ole open-door jeep, and he'd trained his cattle by feeding them piles of sweet pellets so they would follow him from one pasture to the other. The former owner of our property had run the bull with the herd of 125 mama cows year round. Ed taught me that you either had "fall calving" or "spring calving" periods. You segregate the bulls and then decide when you put them in with the herd, allowing them to breed back quicker. We ended up putting the bulls with the heifers

Top, standing, Bill, Ron, and Ellen. Kneeling, Rhonda and Beth. *Bottom,* Edward "Ed" Wadsworth with Ron at Twin Valley, 1983, photography by William McDonald.

on December 1st and with the mature cows on December the 29th; nine months later we had fall calves. Once I started that, I had a defined period where I could check the fertility of the cows. If you have a cow that is not breeding, she has to go. She's not producing. During that period, Ed switched from breeding with Santa Gertrudis bulls to Angus bulls.

For a few years, we held an annual deer hunt at Twin Valley Farms on the first day of the hunting season and invited all the locals to a dinner. Ed was sitting next to me at the table that night, and I said, "Ed, you've had such a phenomenal life you need to write a book and include all the stories." He agreed with me, but I knew he wasn't really going to do it. So in 1983, I hired a writer to interview him, and Twin Valley Press published a book with photos titled *Wadsworth Flats*. We had people come from all over to buy a book at his book-signing party. His grandson, Crawford Jones, recently told me, "I've never seen my grandfather happier than at that book-signing."

In 1986, Beth and I built the first phase of the house. Beth altered the design of a cabin she found in a magazine to suit our needs. She worked with the contractor daily and made the many decisions. Over the years, additions were made, and now "the cabin" has no telling how many square feet. The first additions included a conference room, laundry room, and pool. When our eldest daughter was pregnant with our first grandchild, Beth renovated and enlarged the kitchen and added three more bedrooms and another bathroom. A freestanding building houses our master bedroom, a large screened porch, and a downstairs office, which is connected to the original structure by a "library." Our dear friend Gene Gillespie, who has overseen several of our major projects, handled the construction.

Top, The "cabin," built in 1978. *Bottom left,* Bill and Ron keeping warm, Christmas 1983. *Bottom right,* Bill and Rhonda decorating the tree.

THE HIGH-END ANGUS CATTLE BUSINESS

I soon realized that the costs and the widely vacillating prices of commercial cattle were not going to lead to great profits. In 1985, I bought a few black Angus cattle from a physician friend to quickly increase our Angus population. When we started marketing Angus cattle nationally, we changed the name from REB Ranch to Twin Valley Farms, developed a logo, and produced high-end marketing literature. By 1992, based on the number of calves registered, Beth and I had the largest Angus farm in the Southeast.

Our process of breeding cattle was cutting-edge at that time. We implemented an embryo transfer program in which we placed a purebred embryo in a commercial cow, allowing us to advance several generations in improved genetics. We set up a lab in the barn and used only the best genetic pools. Over the next fifteen years, our cattle evolved from the short, frame-five cow to a taller, frame-seven cow. My thinking was that you got more bone to hang meat on. With the vet attending, we would give the donor cow drugs to make them super-ovulate; sometime they produced fifteen to twenty eggs. The cow has two horns to the uterus, so we'd insert a double cannula catheter, inject a saline solution, and then draw it back out with the embryos included. We'd put them under a microscope, select the eight-cell embryos, and then immediately freeze them. We would then inject the embryos into a common commercial cow, at the correct stage of the estrus cycle, and she would bear a calf that carried all the genetics of the bull and the donor cow. We started doing artificial insemination, as well. As a gynecologist it was right up my alley. The geneticist in me was also intrigued by the process.

Back when I was helping Daddy raise cattle on the homeplace, he had a commercial cow that went into labor but couldn't deliver. As an obstetrician, it sometimes happened that in a human delivery I was presented with a compound presentation, which meant the undelivered baby had a hand down in front of the face or a foot down in front of the butt in a breach delivery. So with this cow, I put my gloved hand in the vagina and I felt these hooves. I called the vet, Chester Gaines, and said, "I've got a compound presentation down here." He came to the barn and just laughed his head off because that's the way calves come, with the feet and nose first. If there was a failed labor, the vet put a cable around each foot, then around a tree and pulled gently. Usually, the cow would survive; the calf not as often. Occasionally, the procedure would injure the cow's nerves going to the pelvis, so after the delivery, it couldn't walk. We'd have to put her down.

TWIN VALLEY FARMS

PRÉ-SALE PARTY

FRIDAY, MAY 16, 1986

PREVIEW OF CATTLE   4:30 - 6:30

COCKTAILS 6:30   DINNER 7:30

Top left, Catalogue for Angus cattle sale at Twin Valley Farms, 1986.
Top right, Twin Valley Farms, signage and flag, 1986. *Bottom left,*
Invitation to buyers for preview of cattle, 1986. *Bottom right,* Top
seller at the 1986 sale was HiLite, selling for $25,000.

At the high point of the Angus business, for almost twelve years, we sold about 150 head of cows the first Saturday of May, the day of the Kentucky Derby. We sold about 350 bulls in November. One year, we had so many bulls we had to split them into three groups. I was out in the pasture counting them and making sure they were all there. I was walking in my cowboy boots, hit a cow pile, fell on my elbow, and tore my rotator cup. It hurt like hell! I put my arm in a sling and didn't sleep a wink that night. My son-in-law, Tom Powell, an outstanding orthopedist, fixed it the next day.

From the beginning, we only dealt in high-grade genetics. People from all over the country began coming to buy bulls from us. We operated on an annual budget of $2.5 million or more. There were two potential markets: selling Angus cows with a calf inside for $17,500–$20,000, or selling the recipient commercial cow with the embryo for $7,500. We sold many cow-calf pairs for $20,000 and one bull for $51,000. We developed a national network of cattle farmers from the Southeast, New England, Ohio, and California and maintained a mutually beneficial relationship with three main farms. Those fifteen years were a charmed period in the financial life of Twin Valley Farms, LLC.

It was also a joyous time for our family, all of whom played a part. On sale days, the whole family was involved, eventually even the children's spouses. Beth, Bill, and I functioned as hosts. Rhonda's husband, Tommy, was often the chauffer for out-of-town guests. Ellen and Rhonda registered buyers and checked them out after the sale, keeping records of lots sold and prices paid. Bill's wife, Lyn, always sat in the auctioneer's box and recorded buyer's numbers and sale prices for each lot. As the grandchildren came along, we would hire a babysitter to watch them. They were always at the barn at the beginning of the sale to be introduced as "the next generation."

Top left, Beth standing on the back deck, overlooking the pond, 1989. *Top right,* Ron with John Deere tractor, 1989. *Bottom left,* The "cabin" in 1989. *Bottom right,* Ron preparing for the Spirit Cattle Sale, 1989.

Top, Cattle sale, 1990. *Center:* Back row, (from left): Tommy Powell, Bill, and Ron. Front: Rhonda, Ellen, and Beth, 1990. *Bottom:* Sara "Granny" Henderson, Willie Mae Frey, Elizabeth "Mamaw" Summerville, and Mrs. Rodger sign up bidders at the sale.

TWIN VALLEY

Annual Breeding Age Bull Sale

11:00 A.M. C.S.T.
Saturday, November 7, 1992

At the Farm near
Prattville, Alabama

Top left, The award-winning sale barn at Twin Valley Farms, 1992. *Top right,* Program. *Right center,* Top-seller Miss Blackcap sold for $5,800, 1992. *Bottom left,* The sale cow and calf in ring, 1992. *Bottom right,* Tommy, Rhonda, Ellen, Lyn, and Bill, 1992.

FRIENDS MADE IN THE CATTLE BUSINESS

Beth and I traveled all over the country with the cattle business, sometimes flying our own plane, and really enjoyed it. We also loved entertaining at the farm. We met a lot of fantastic people, such as Jim Coleman, the son-in-law of Julio Gallo of the Gallo Wines family from Modesto, California. Jim and his wife visited our farm and bought cattle from us. Beth and I went to Modesto and spent the night in the couple's beautiful home. They had a walk-in refrigerator as big as two rooms. But they're just nice, salt-of-the-earth people.

Dave Bittner and his wife, Nancy, own and operate Silver Plume Ranch in Paxton, Nebraska, where they breed Angus cattle. Former executives of the Monsanto Company, the multinational agrochemical and agricultural biotechnology corporation, Dave and Nancy are both extremely intelligent and function as a team. During our Angus breeding days, Dave called and wanted to come to a TVF cattle sale. We hosted Nancy and him for a weekend, and we've been friends ever since. Dave is very goal oriented, always experimenting with cattle and feed yards. At eighty years old, he is currently interested in the conversion rate of grain to beef. He is conducting a food absorption study where he measures the food cows eat from the feed yard and what they convert to meat.

We also got to know Frank Vandersloot from Idaho Falls, Idaho, who founded and is CEO of a direct sales company called Melaleuca, Inc. Frank, a Mormon, served as Mitt Romney's national finance co-chair in his 2008 and 2012 presidential bids. Back in the late 1980s, Frank was just getting started in the cattle business and had seen the TVF catalogs. He called me and bought $350,000 worth of my cattle based on my recommendation, before I even met him. It was a real compliment, but it put a lot of pressure on me, handpicking an entire herd. I also helped him find a competent manager because at that time he didn't know much about working cattle.

Frank invited Beth and me to Idaho Falls, which is about ninety percent Mormon. We spent one night in their enormous home. His wife had been married before, and combined they had seventeen children. When the kids came downstairs to dinner, they sat around the table and were "seen but not heard." Frank has a brilliant mind and is driven, willing to take risk. He ended up with a beautiful Angus business, Riverbend Ranch, one of the largest purebred and commercial cattle operations in the country. He really knew how to market it. I think Frank is a model of a good citizen. As an entrepreneur, radio network owner, and rancher, he has made a lot of money; but he spends it right, investing in what he believes.

In 1989, I met a stockbroker, Tim Russell, from Palmerston North, New Zealand, at a Denver cattlemen's show. He and his wife, Karen, later came to visit us at the farm. We had steaks, and Tim suggested I take a trip to New Zealand. He knew of a twelve-thousand-acre farm or "station" dedicated to the grazing of fifteen hundred cows and fifteen thousand sheep. A few months later, Beth and I flew to Fiji, and I was to go on to New Zealand to investigate. At dinner in the hotel restaurant the first night in Fiji, a tall, bald-headed guy was standing nearby talking to a waiter. I said, "Beth, he sounds like us!" So I went over and introduced myself to Harry P. Williams. He was intelligent, upbeat, and gregarious, and I liked him instantly. Harry had built an insurance company in Spartanburg, South Carolina. As an insurance salesman he knew a lot of jokes and stories! Harry and his wife, Betsy, sort of adopted Beth when I went on to New Zealand to check out the land.

Top left, Ron with Nancy and Dave Bittner at the TVF 1990 cattle sale. *Top right,* Betsy and Harry P. Williams at Rhonda's wedding, Birmingham, Alabama, 1991. *Left,* Betsy, Ron, Carmen Habeeb, and Harry at TVF, 1991.

In New Zealand, the grandson of the British ranch owner toured me all over those hills of the farm, called Erohorn, in his grandfather's old Cadillac. He introduced me to the somewhat seedy farm manager, whom I didn't particularly like. They showed me all the financials, with revenue that would have allowed for me to pay for it in eight years. We dined with the owners, in very British fashion, with all of us seated just so. I was to the left of the host. The Erohorn homeplace was situated on the crest of a mountain, and you could see for miles—it was just very seductive.

But I ran the details past my advisor in New York, and he said, "Doctor, let me tell you, this is *doable*, but the New Zealand economy is such a small thing, if it goes downhill, you're going to be in trouble." The purchase also challenged the sanity of owning property on the other side of the world! Beth and I decided that since our family was back in the States, we wouldn't have stayed there much, maybe once a year, if that. Beth wasn't in favor of it, and I finally turned it down. Three years later, all hell broke loose with New Zealand's economy, so it was a good decision.

After the trip, we continued to visit with the Williams at their place on Lake Summit in North Carolina or at Twin Valley Farms. On our last visit to see Harry at the lake, Betsy had been moved to a memory care center, where he visits her daily. Harry, who is now ninety-three years old, recently called me and said, "Son, you can't believe what I did today! I jumped out of an airplane at twelve thousand feet." With some people, it's just good to be in their presence. He's just smart and fun to be around. He has gone through a lot of hard stuff in his life, but he hasn't stopped being himself. He is one of my inspirations for living a long, fulfilling life—he is in good health, exercises in the pool, and still drives.

We also have found good friends among the colorful characters who keep Twin Valley Farms operating, our employees. Mac Mitchell, who was about sixty-nine when I met him, was born, raised, and died on the farm. Mac lived in an old shack of a house with a hand-dug well in the front yard on Highway 41. I would hire him to do odd jobs on the farm. Using old railroad ties, Mac and I made steps leading up to what was the trailer and is now the house, and also descending to the pond. I like the idea of putting the *old* with the *new*. But Mac was a pal of mine—he'd light up when he saw me, and I'd brag on him. Just a nice guy. He died at eighty-two years of age.

We've had a succession of farm managers, some tenures more successful than others. The first potential candidate, a retired accountant, showed up uninvited at the trailer at 7 a.m. one weekend. The two of us got in our Jeep to tour the property. As passenger, it was his job to open the "gaps," temporary gates made of barbed wire and poles, as we didn't have gates yet. He opened the first gap, I drove through, and he closed the gap; but he was on the wrong side of the gap. I showed him a couple of things, drove back home, and said, "I'll call ya."

We eventually hired a rough and ready man named Eddie Brown, who was crazy about horses, which we had at the time. As we moved more toward a major cattle operation, Eddie moved on, and we replaced him with David Nordine, from Iowa, who knew more about cattle. As we began to specialize in Angus cattle, we hired Bobby Freeman, an Auburn graduate in agriculture science, who made a lot of positive steps in the selection of Angus cattle. Working closely with the veterinarians, Bobby helped establish the embryo transfer and artificial insemination programs. The best fit for a manager we ever had was Roland Starns, a hard worker and capable leader of men. Roland stayed with us for twelve years and could just do it all. He has a true love for cattle and a knack for the breeding, the genetics, just the whole nine yards.

In 2004, we decided to get out of the cattle business. That year, we had the main dispersal, selling all the equipment and most all the cattle. I kept some purebred heifers but sold the last of them in 2006.

TWIN VALLEY FARMS TODAY

There is an old saying, "You can take the boy out of country, but you can't take the country out of the boy." And I've never left it—I am particularly tied to the land and cattle. Crawford Jones, the grandson of my mentor, Ed Wadsworth, has leased the majority of land and farming facilities at Twin Valley Farms, LLC. Recently, he and his crew have assumed the duties of maintaining the entire farm, which is a vast improvement on my former situation of employing a farm manager. In his forties, Crawford is just like his grandfather, industrious and intelligent. He and his brother Cooper work out of the same banking account and live right next door to each other. He leases my property to run his cows and grow and cut hay; and he has complete run of the property and equipment.

In 2010, I helped Crawford write a structured business plan that he is still following. He is a born leader and is very organized in his approach to teamwork. He has four full-time employees that he directs continually, and he recently hired a much-needed assistant manager for his operation. He has mandatory 4 p.m. daily meetings to discuss problems, progress, and opportunities.

Crawford has taken the initiative to enhance the functionality and the appearance of Twin Valley. In 2012, he rented an excavator for a month and removed all the brush and small trees from the edge of the pastures. He keeps up the fencing and the ground cover and fills the low places with gravel. Crawford's successful breeding and marketing of cattle, as well as cultivation of hay for use and for sale, has been a beautiful thing to watch. Our friendship has been and continues to be an evolving and strengthening Christian relationship.

Most of the things I've done have been motivated by practical reasons, with a mission in mind. I feel that the Lord put me here for a reason, to magnify him and manifest his glory through faith, family, and friends. If you look around, there are a lot of successful people who are sitting on their laurels. I don't want to do that. My business cards read, "Ronald E. Henderson: Physician, Author, Entrepreneur." I don't want to ever stop fostering ideas and projects. I think when you stop trying, you start dying.

The profit from the Angus operation allowed us to build a $250,000 building that evolved from functioning as a sale barn to what is now "The Barn at Twin Valley Farms," an events center. My daughter-in-law, Lyn Henderson, is events director, responsible for leasing and overseeing the entire operation, a job she does mostly from their home in Vestavia Hills. Crawford and his

Top, The house at Twin Valley Farms today.
Bottom left, Crawford Jones, neighbor,
friend, and farm manager, 2014. *Bottom
right,* The former show barn at TVF is now
an events space.

team are there to assist her when needed. We can seat 250 people for a meal, and have a stage with dual audio systems for performances, weddings, and reunions.

This past Fourth of July, we hosted forty-seven members of the Henderson family at a reunion at Twin Valley Farms. No fewer than twelve children went swimming in the pool. Now we've got walking and riding trails and gardens on the tiered hills. We've got all these toys for young people to play with: a four-seat all-terrain vehicle called a Ranger, two four-wheelers, a tram, an electric golf cart, and a gasoline golf cart.

Beth and I retreat to the farm as often as possible. We pick blueberries when in season and walk the trails. I have always valued land because my Daddy taught me the importance of it at an early age. Daddy was the first-born male of six children, and all of his family was impressed because he was a landowner. He was proud of that. Our first year in Gordo, in 1964, Beth and I bought half interest in the homeplace. I guess it was always in the back of my mind that I wanted to build a large farm. Not just for the farming but for the land itself. Now we have about seventeen hundred acres including the homeplace. And they're not making any more land, so it's a good investment. The most satisfying part is that the kids and grandkids like to come and bring their friends. They're proud of it, too. What is happening now makes my heart sing. I tell them, "We built this for you." It is Eden—just beautiful.

Top, Henderson Family Reunion at Twin Valley Farms, 2013. *Bottom left,* from left, back: Caroline, Lauren, Matthew, and Katie. Front: James and Maggie at TVF. *Bottom right,* from left: Lauren, James, Caroline, Katie, Matthew, and Maggie, 2013.

JOURNAL

of the Medical Association of the State of Alabama

VOL. 51, NO. 10 APRIL, 1982

MASA's New President:
What Makes Dr. Henderson Run?

Journal of the Medical Association of the State of Alabama, Vol. 51, No. 10, April 1982.
(continued on page 188)

CHAPTER 8

ENTREPRENEURIAL EFFORTS

1968–1997

As the president of the State Medical Association in 1982, I was interviewed by a writer who asked, essentially, "What makes you tick?" My response was to explain the "Three R's of Ron Henderson." Most of us are driven by three things, in varying degrees: Romance, Recognition, and Remuneration. I am primarily driven by romance. I do something because it's attractive to me, because I enjoy it—if I don't enjoy it, I don't do it. I don't care about the recognition. I try to accept recognition graciously when I do something special, but I don't go looking for it. And of course, remuneration, making money, is necessary but not the reason I spring out of bed in the morning. I think my faith has helped me to maintain my priorities and to structure my career for the right reasons. As a physician, the patient always came first. I have lived by that, I have taught that, and anybody under my management who forgot that rule was gone. And I have been extremely blessed financially. If you keep your faith, and follow a defined business plan, God takes care of you.

For me, the business itself holds an element of romance in that it is challenging and interesting—it is the romance of *improving the system.* My actions should always increase value in every effort. Many people have told me that few doctors are business people. Apparently, it is rare to have it all in one package. God gave me a lot of useful talents and a lot of energy. The ability to lead by example and to convince others to follow is a magical gift, and it's not that hard. You have to know your own limitations and be able to select quality people to work with you. You've got to make sure to continually monitor everything that is going on at all levels. For instance, I distributed a patient survey once a quarter so I could get feedback on the doctors and whether the patients were happy or not. And if a doctor wasn't holding up his or her end of the deal, I would set up a meeting to review the survey. The patients loved it, and the surveys gave us basic information that we needed for continual improvement of the service that we delivered. And all our physicians showed major improvement in the areas involved.

In 1987, I ran for the American Medical Association Board of Trustees with the ultimate goal of running for president. My two main supporters, a plastic surgeon from Phoenix, Arizona, and an orthopedist from Huntsville, Alabama, did not show up for the elections in Chicago. I got beat by one vote. On my return flight back home, I was very discouraged and upset. When we hit the turbulent weather over Tennessee, the plane suddenly went up and came down, and a nun seated on my left landed right in my lap. It was the Lord at work. I asked myself, *What in the world am I doing here?* I came home and resigned from all AMA activities and began focusing on my entrepreneurial work, none of which would have occurred if I had stayed on that track.

When I first went into practice on my own in Birmingham I was using the traditional eyeshade accountant. As my entrepreneurial efforts became more ambitious, everybody kept telling me to go see the accountant Paul Kassouf and the lawyer Harold Apolinsky of Serote & Permutt. Friends warned that I might not get in to see them because they were in such demand. I went to see both of them independently; they both spoke highly of each other and seemed to work as a successful team. They just really understood business and made a vital difference to my endeavors, Paul on the accounting side and Harold on the legal side. When I started each of my entrepreneurial activities, they were closely involved from the outset. Financially, they put me on the map. I didn't do a thing business-wise unless they signed off on it. They were expensive, but you get what you pay for and they were worth every penny.

A CONVERSATION WITH RON HENDERSON

Candidate for the
AMA Board of Trustees

Top, Ron speaks before the American Medical Association membership. *Bottom,* A brochure and button produced for Ron's campaign for the American Medical Association Board of Trustees, 1987.

BUILDING THE HENDERSON & WALTON WOMEN'S CENTER, 1968–1994

Dr. Philip Walton joined our practice, Henderson & Moore, in 1976. Tall, smart, and charismatic, Phil was one of my former residents. Ernie, Phil, and I could attract more patients than we could possibly see. We made a remarkable professional team, and our practice exploded. We soon had to figure out how to enlarge the office.

In 1982, we recruited Drs. John Faucett and Charles Hudson from the Carraway Methodist Medical Center to join our practice. Both talented doctors, they brought many patients with them, and the practice continued to grow. Soon after, we hired Dr. Frank Page—very intelligent, high energy, and extremely driven, one the most highly recruited physicians in the Southeast.

I was always looking for an entrepreneurial approach to anything that I was involved with and saw this rapid growth as a great opportunity. From 1987 through 1992, we grew from a five-person practice to nineteen physicians, divided into three teams for patient care. We built satellite offices in Cullman, Anniston, Sylacauga, Alabaster, Tuscaloosa, Gadsden, and Jasper, all about fifty miles from Birmingham. Having the satellite offices so close made it convenient for patients to get their primary care close to home and receive their tertiary care—some of which was available in our offices, such as ultrasounds and mammography—and receive major surgery and hospitalizations at St. Vincent's Hospital in Birmingham.

Frank Page had been at the University of Mississippi Medical College in Jackson, Mississippi, and had many contacts there. This allowed us to recruit Drs. Cindy Lassiter, Beth Snowden, and John Woods from Jackson. We also brought on board Dr. Carol Swindle, originally from Jasper, Alabama, with an outstanding clinical education at Vanderbilt University in Nashville, Tennessee, along with another Vanderbilt graduate in medical education (who was later terminated due to quality of care issues), and Dr. Jeff Gunnels, who received his residency training at the University of South Alabama in Mobile. A physician practicing in Anniston, Dr. Charles Brockwell, was with us for a little over a year but went back to Anniston for family reasons.

Beth and I had moved our family to a house on Old Leeds Road in 1983, and potential hires and their spouses would come spend the night with us in our home. We'd either cook steak or carry them out to dinner. I wanted to see the chemistry between the couple, and I wanted to see the chemistry

Top left, June Zealy, Wilma Conner, Ron, staff member, Mildred Scarborough, and Donna Weems, 1976.
Top right, Ernie, Ron, and Phil at the office in St. Vincent's Hospital, Professional Building 1, 1976.
Bottom, Ron speaking at the American Medical Association Conference in Chicago, Illinois, 1978.

between them and me. We invited all of them to our home, and I knew right away if the hire was going to work out long-term or not. In a rapid growth phase, sometimes you are forced to make compromises if you're a leader. You may need to go forward with an imperfect situation, knowing it is a mistake, in order to build, and then you correct it as soon as you can. You've got to be able to adjust.

As a doctor, I have always lived by and taught the Four C's of Medical Care—the care must be Competent, Compassionate, Convenient, and Cost-Effective. We insisted that the doctors in our practice abide by this code of ethics. The practice style that we promoted was straightforward; as a doctor, you had to demonstrate that you cared about your patients. If you're gonna take care of patients, you've got to have it in your *head* and your *heart* that you genuinely care about their well-being. Otherwise, you shouldn't be there. There were only a couple of doctors who fell short of this code of ethics, and we had to let them go.

The remaining staff members were all fantastic doctors and true professionals. We had just surrounded ourselves with brilliant people. At that time, our practice had grown so big that UAB doctors were nervous about joining an operation so expansive and busy. The doctors who came from Mississippi didn't have that perception. And they all worked hard. They were the nucleus of that explosive growth, opening up all the satellites.

As a chief executive officer, I considered myself the *bottom rock* in an inverted pyramid. As a leader, my role is to enhance the function of the entire organization by giving my associates not only responsibilities but also the authority to implement those responsibilities. This inverted pyramid is magical beyond words when it is properly done.

Belinda Cornelius had been a practice manager for five cardiologists in Florida and then worked at Children's Hospital in Birmingham. In 1988, she applied for a position at Henderson & Walton, and I was so impressed with her that I interviewed her at least three times. She was bright, high-energy, positive, and never met a stranger—she had people skills coming out of every pore. I had found this diamond in the rough that I desperately wanted to work with me. However, I didn't really have a place for her. Gayle Kirkland, RN, was my practice administrator and was doing a fantastic job. Belinda was overqualified for the available position, but I hired her anyway in a newly created accounting capacity.

At that time, all of the expenses and revenues for the practice were managed on paper, and I asked Belinda to oversee the computerization of all the

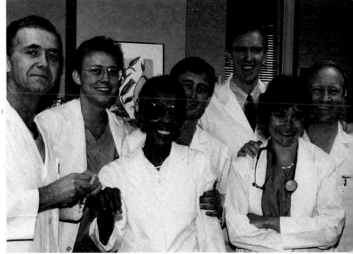

Top left, front, from left: Pat Miller, Ron, Donna Weems, and Charles Hudson. Back, from left: Randy Yarborough, Frank Page, and Phil Walton. *Top right,* The Henderson's house on Old Leeds Road, 1990. *Bottom left,* Henderson, Moore, and Walton, staff Christmas party, 1979. *Bottom right,* front, from left: Ron, Wilma Conner, and Pat Miller. Back: Randy Yarborough, Frank Page, Phil Walton, and Charles Hudson.

records. We had just opened the Cullman satellite, and Belinda assumed the lead role in the start-up of operations for the new satellites. She had solid experience setting up orthopedic offices for Children's Hospital. Belinda became so adept at facilitating the start-up of the satellites that it became almost reflexive. Using our new software, she was able to track the expenses and revenues of each satellite so that we were able to determine profitability. Each satellite had to stand on its own feet and be profitable. Belinda had an early Macintosh computer and lugged the hard drive tower from place to place because everything had to be manually entered. She also computerized the finances at Twin Valley Farms, LLC, tracking revenue and expenses. At her first cattle auction, Belinda was bewildered because buyers were bidding but there was nothing in the show ring. I explained to her that the buyers were bidding on the semen from some of our outstanding Angus bulls.

The satellite implementation plan, which we all became good at facilitating, was to first find an office to rent with a long-term lease or location to build. To practice basic primary care, all we needed was a reception area and at least three treatment rooms. The patients we were already seeing brought more patients, which brought more revenue back to the central practice, in particular for the ultrasounds and mammographies. Having the association with St. Vincent's Hospital, a well-known, respected institution, was a *huge* factor in our success. Everybody loves a Catholic hospital. If you've ever been in one, you can just feel the difference.

We were able to pull off such an ambitious satellite expansion quickly because Ernie, Phil, Frank, and I developed a foolproof method of passing decisions in the executive meetings. Prior to the meeting, I made sure they knew which way I wanted to go. Phil would make the motion, Frank would second it, and I'd call for the question, "Any opposition?" No. It went right through. That is how we built the satellites—my partners' support was critical.

Above, Henderson & Walton
Women's Center staff party, 1989.

Branding the Practice

Around 1987, I brought in a marketing guy from Montgomery to advise us on branding the practice as a whole. At that time, the name of the operation was Henderson, Moore & Walton. My friend Ernie had moved on to a private gynecology practice of his own. But we had fifteen doctors, and everybody wanted their names included. The marketing guy said, "You can't have all the doctors' names." We whittled it down to "Henderson & Walton." The marketing guy said it needed to speak large—not practice, not office, but *Center*. So we named it the Henderson & Walton Women's Center. We got the logo created; it was a great template and is still in use at St. Vincent's today.

The communities where our satellites were located were desperate for medical care. From 1987 through 1992, our patients and referrals were the difference between St. Vincent's going out of business, like St. Margaret's in Montgomery did, and black ink. The CFO at that time, Curtis James, told me, "Dr. Henderson, if you hadn't created those satellites, we wouldn't have survived." During that time, we were getting revenue from the ultra-sounds, X-rays, and particularly for the surgery and the obstetrics. We were delivering from 185 to 200 babies a month. We also referred our patients to physicians on St. Vincent's medical staff for internal medicine, general surgery, orthopedics, and neurosurgery. It was exciting—and the patients and the hospital appreciated what we were doing.

In the late '80s, St. Vincent's Hospital in Birmingham received accreditation from the Joint Commission on Accreditation of Healthcare Organizations. Soon after, I called the Chicago-based organization to ask about the possibility of them inspecting Henderson & Walton for accreditation. The staff person asked, "Now *where* are you?" I said, "Birmingham, Alabama." He then asked, "You want us to come there and do what?" And I said, "We are a private ob-gyn practice in Birmingham, Alabama, and we would like to stand for inspection to achieve accreditation." He set a date, and their inspectors spent four days in our practice, a tremendous undertaking for our physicians and particularly our administrative staff. I had forewarned our staff that this was going to be a rigorous process—they put their shoulders to the plow and made it happen. In 1990, we received an "Accreditation with Commendation" designation from the Joint Commission on Accreditation of Healthcare Organizations. We were the first private practice in the United States to achieve accreditation. It was one of the proudest moments of my professional career.

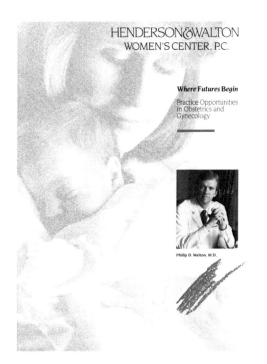

HENDERSON&WALTON
WOMEN'S CENTER, P.C.

Where Futures Begin

Practice Opportunities
in Obstetrics and
Gynecology

Philip D. Walton, M.D.

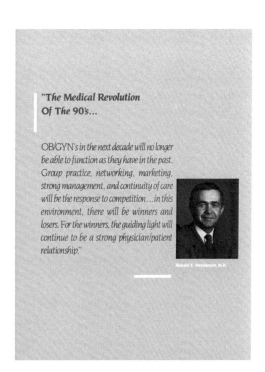

**"The Medical Revolution
Of The 90's...**

OB/GYN's in the next decade will no longer
be able to function as they have in the past.
Group practice, networking, marketing,
strong management, and continuity of care
will be the response to competition...in this
environment, there will be winners and
losers. For the winners, the guiding light will
continue to be a strong physician/patient
relationship."

Ronald E. Henderson, M.D.

Top, Literature created as part of the rebranding effort for Henderson & Walton Women's Center, 1991.
Bottom, Henderson & Walton Women's Center staff Christmas party, early '90s.

MUTUAL ASSURANCE (PROASSURANCE), 1976–1986

In 1974, my partner Ernie was sued by a plaintiff's lawyer representing a woman claiming "wrongful life." An unstable woman, a thirty-six-year-old traveling quilter, came to Ernie with a pregnancy. She wanted a boy; she did not want a female child. So she asked Ernie to conduct an amniocentesis test to determine the sex of the child, and he refused. An amniocentesis test is primarily a prenatal test to check for chromosomal abnormalities. She had passed the time in which the test could be done for this reason. She delivered a baby with Down syndrome and sued Ernie.

By that time, two fellow physicians and I had founded a mutual professional liability insurance company called Mutual Assurance. I sat on the claims committee, with other physicians, to determine whether a suit brought against a doctor was actually malpractice or malfeasance as claimed. If it wasn't malpractice or malfeasance, instead of settling, we defended the doctor. Our mantra was "Deny and Defend." We were trying to protect our doctors against all-fronts assaults from plaintiffs' lawyers. Our solid stance diminished the onslaught of groundless attacks and created a better environment for doctors.

At first, my friend Ernie wanted to settle his case. I said, "No, we're not going to settle this; we're going to defend." The trial went on for more than ten days. On Wednesday of the second week, it finally went to the jury, which stayed out for seventeen minutes and ruled in his favor. Three of the women on the jury started coming to Ernie as their ob-gyn.

However, that experience made Ernie a target for all the plaintiffs' lawyers in the Birmingham area. Many unfounded suits were filed against him, and after about a year of Ernie dealing with suit after suit, he decided that he must give up obstetrics and practice gynecology. Ernie was a great doctor, but he knew he was a lightning rod for these plaintiffs' lawyers, which undermined his ability to practice obstetrics. He happily moved to his own office the next month. His wife, Sue, served as a receptionist, bookkeeper, and advisor for a while, which brought them even closer together, toward a common purpose. From then on, he had a fantastic career practicing gynecology. Ernie and I are friends to this day and talk often. He is an outstanding person with a strong moral compass, and a darn good doctor. And I love him like a brother.

Henderson Is Honored By The AMA

The American Medical Association House of Delegates elected four physicians, two of them incumbents, to the AMA Council on Medical Service at the Association's annual meeting last week. Each term lasts three years.

A newcomer to the council is Ronald E. Henderson, an obstetrician and gynecologist from Birmingham. Henderson is a native of Prattville, and still operates a farm in the county.

Henderson was recently elected president of the Alabama State Medical Association. He has been chief of obstetrics and gynecology at St. Vincent's Hospital since 1970.

He is in private practice and holds staff appointments at the University of Alabama Hospitals and Clinics, Baptist, Brookwood and St. Vincent's Hospitals.

He received his MD degree from UAB in 1962 and now serves the school as clinical assistant professor of medicine.

ROTARY GRAMS
OFFICIAL PUBLICATION CLUB NUMBER FIFTY-SIX
BIRMINGHAM, ALABAMA
HOME OF TWO INTERNATIONAL PRESIDENTS

TODAY
SEPTEMBER 22

Rotarian
RONALD E. HENDERSON, M.D.
"ECONOMICS OF MEDICAL CARE"

SPECIAL INTERNATIONAL EDITION
HATS OFF TO THE BRIDGE BUILDERS

This issue contains mention of a number of 'bridge builders' . . . in both community and international service . . . see how many you can identify!

Above top and right, Campaign paraphernalia for Ron's run for the Council on Medical Service for the American Medical Association, Chicago, 1982. *Bottom left,* Ron spoke to downtown Birmingham Rotary Club on the "Economics of Medical Care," 1982.

In 1991, we converted Mutual Assurance to a public company called Pro-Assurance and made an initial public offering (IPO). The CEO at that time, A. Derrill Crowe, MD, and I split the excess stock (that which had not been purchased by the other physicians) on a fifty-fifty basis to facilitate the IPO. The very day it went public, the stock went from $10 to $17 dollars a share and is now about $45 per share. Each covered physician was awarded $10,000 at the time of the IPO. I had bought the stock from three of my colleagues for $10,000 each. I offered all three the opportunity to have the stock at $17.50 per share, but they all declined because they felt like they had made a deal and needed to stick by it. It was a true windfall for Crowe and me.

THE BIRMINGHAM SURGICAL CENTER, 1983–1994

In 1983, I spearheaded another entrepreneurial effort, the Birmingham Surgical Center, the first freestanding outpatient surgical care facility in the Southeast. The first outpatient surgical clinic in the country was started by an anesthesiologist in Phoenix, Arizona. At that time, the prevailing opinion was that a surgical patient needed to be in the hospital for availability of blood and aesthesia. The anesthesiologist in Phoenix was a real visionary. He realized that he could be more efficient in the outpatient setting because he ran the schedule, so everything flowed better. I traveled to Phoenix to check out their setup and within three months had formed a Birmingham committee that included the anesthesiologist Dr. Bebo Fitzpatrick, who would be the chief of staff. I was one of the seven founding members. Five of us worked together to raise the money and build the outpatient clinic.

In a hospital, you get tied up with all kinds of bureaucracy and schedules. At the Center, I had a surgery day and would do three operations in the time it'd take to do one at the hospital. If I needed to add a case I scheduled it at noon. Most hospitals started at 7 a.m., but I moved our first surgery back to 6 a.m. I'd do a vaginal hysterectomy at 6 a.m., put 'em in the recovery room, and then I would go by to see 'em at 5 p.m. and send 'em home. Everybody asked, "You sent a major surgery home?" I said, "Well, they're stable." We never had a problem. Drs. Walton and Page still tease me, saying, "You'd go down there and do two D&Cs and you wouldn't even turn your car off." And I *would* line up patients in back-to-back rooms, so it wouldn't take long—but I did turn off my car. Patients loved it. I loved it.

Ronald E. Henderson, M.D.
20th Anniversary
Relay House
June 30, 1988
"A Roast to Remember"

Cocktails and Hor' doeuvres 7:00
Special Program 8:00

Host
Philip D. Walton, M.D.

Special Presentation
Frank O. Page, M.D.

Honored Speakers
Harold Apolinsky
William Dodson, M.D.
Alfred Habeeb, M.D.
Sonny Housel
Paul Kassouf
Ernie Moore, M.D.

Special Presentation
Gayle Kirkland, R.N.
Practice Manager

Above, Ron's Twentieth-Year Anniversary Roast, 1988.

The hospital, however, didn't like it one bit; they really complained. The Center was ultimately instrumental in driving down costs of outpatient surgical procedures and pushing hospitals to open same-day surgical units.

Another impetus to get the Surgical Center established was the fact that as a Catholic hospital, St. Vincent's wouldn't allow sterilizations and was losing obstetric patients because of its inability to perform tubal ligations. Once the Surgical Center was built, I would deliver the baby at St. Vincent's, and on the second post-partum day, I would give the patient a leave of absence and a family member would take her to the Surgical Center. After recovering from the tubal ligation, the family member would bring her back to the hospital. It still works to this day, proving there's more than one way to skin a cat!

I'd had several entrepreneurial endeavors, but the Surgical Center was the first bonanza for me. The thing *kept* making money and making money. Eventually, a company in Nashville wanted to buy it, and we really cashed out big. The original five investors turned a large profit on their investments. We included all kinds of caveats in the deal to keep the quality high. One was that our chief anesthesiologist, Dr. Bebo Fitzpatrick, would continue as the manager of the Surgical Center. Everybody won—the doctors, patients, and insurance companies.

I know I've been successful, but it's not me—I'm a tool of the Lord. He's given me these skills, and he wants me to use them right. He doesn't want me to mess up. That's my driver, my motivation. If there is even a possibility that he would be unhappy, I don't do it. A committee to discuss abortions was formed at UAB, and as chairman of the ob-gyn department at St. Vincent's, I was asked to serve. So I went to the sister in charge and said, "I think I should take part in this, Sister, because we've got to have a voice over there." At that time, if a patient insisted on an abortion, I had the front desk give her the number to an abortion clinic in Atlanta. I just never felt right about performing abortions myself. It is an interesting issue, still under debate: Whether the right of the born supersedes the right of the unborn. In a rape or incest case, or an extremely defective baby, you can make the case to justify an abortion. Other than that, to end a normal pregnancy, it's hard to make that case. As an ob-gyn physician, you've just got to set your own standards and hold to 'em. To this day, I am a "right-to-life" physician.

Ron and Beth dressed for the President's Ball at St. Vincent's Hospital, Kennesaw Drive, 1983.

SOUTHEAST HEALTH PLAN, INC., 1984–1991

In 1984, I started a physician-owned health maintenance organization (HMO) called Southeast Health Plan. I had learned about the concept from a colleague in California, a pediatrician by the name of Robert Burnett. I was serving as vice chairman on the Council of Medical Services at the American Medical Association (AMA), and Dr. Burnett, the chairman, was often absent, which meant I chaired the committee. He and some colleagues were starting a physician-owned HMO in California. The HMO was initially designed to give the patient the tools to maintain his or her health by providing managed care and to act as a liaison between providers (doctors and hospitals) and third-party payers (insurance companies).

Of all of my entrepreneurial efforts, I'd never done anything this much from scratch; but I thought if they could do it in California, we could do it here in Alabama. I literally started with a clean sheet of paper. Like my other efforts, Southeast Health Plan (SEHP) was an attempt to fill a need or rectify a substandard system. Third-party payers, the insurance companies, don't think as much about the patient as the doctors do—our focus is on the patient. United Health, Aetna, Blue Cross—all the insurance companies— were based on models with a top priority of making money.

As founder, I started raising capital, building a board, and hiring staff. I brought in George B. Salem from Methodist Hospital in Memphis as chief executive officer, and I remained chairman of the board. George was extremely competent and highly sought after, even as a young man. In Memphis, he managed hospital operations and was part of a highly successful hospital acquisition team. For medical director, I hired Richard McLaughlin, MD, away from Carraway Methodist Medical Hospital in Jefferson County. Richard is a great guy who loved talking to the doctors about their habits. I brought in the talented Nan Priest, whom I had promoted from a nurse in the labor and delivery room to the practice administrator at Henderson & Walton Women's Center, as vice president of managed care. This was a major sacrifice on my part because Nan did such a great job as my practice administrator. Tony Crowe, who had been my assistant when I was president of the Medical Association of the State of Alabama, came on as a development person. These were my first four hires.

In the early '70s, Richard "Rich" Burke started an HMO in the Southwest that became United Healthcare. He was probably the most financially successful person in the HMO industry. I met Rich Burke in the early days of starting SEHP, through the cattle business. I had explained my plans for SEHP, and he thought it was perfect for Alabama. On one of his visits to

Birmingham, I invited Rich and George to have dinner with us when we lived on Old Leeds Road. We sat by the swimming pool, drinking a glass of wine in absolutely gorgeous weather, looking out over a crest view. George was still trying to decide whether to accept our position of CEO because he had been offered a job in a Houston hospital. Rich said to George, "You need to take this job because I know these people and they're going to do it the correct way." That was one of the many reasons George came on board as CEO. He took a risk signing on with a startup company, but he was ready for a more innovative, dynamic position.

By the time George got here, I had already made good headway assembling an incredible board of top-flight doctors to represent different geographical areas within the community. To raise the needed capital, I put in $25,000, each board member put in $10,000, and each doctor put in $5,000 minimum. Several doctors put in more than $5,000, thinking they were going to get preferential treatment. But everybody got treated the same.

We had representation from all the key hospitals on our board. And it was an intensely *committed* board. In the first month, we had a board meeting every day at 6 a.m. and the committees met at 5 a.m. About twenty days into it, I think George was asking himself, "What the hell have I gotten myself into? These guys are crazy!" We were putting more effort into it than our competitors. Although ours was the first HMO to start up in the state, within a year there were twelve others. We eventually absorbed three of them after they got into trouble.

From the outset, we never intended the company to be a huge moneymaker for investors to line their pockets. We wanted to generate a plan that was cash-flow positive but also to make sure that we addressed the patients' needs by altering how the patients took care of themselves and how providers, doctors, and hospitals handled quality and costs.

The health-care system in this country takes a beating because it's the most expensive system in the world. But the fact of the matter is, there is a patient responsibility here, too. We're the most obese country in the world. Decade by decade, studies show Americans getting fatter, and the trend in Alabama is growing at an astounding rate. Nothing good comes from too much weight: diabetes, cancer, heart and cholesterol issues. We have a lot of sick people in this country. Americans have the mindset that they can eat what they want and not exercise—then when something goes wrong, the medical system will fix it. Our philosophy was that we were going to try to *alter the behavior of the patient* and have them take more responsibility for themselves. We would give them the tools to do it by lowering copays for physicals, mammograms, and all the necessary screenings. We also published educational materials to support this philosophy.

The other part of our philosophy was to also try to *alter practice patterns.* A well-run HMO is the best care the patient's going to get anywhere because there are so many safeguards in place to ensure quality care that aren't there in standard indemnity insurance. The typical patient is just not knowledgeable enough to appreciate that. We worked hard to credential and hold doctors to agreed-upon high standards. In this state, we were pioneering new trails in health care and it was exciting.

We did a lot of things differently than our competitors—we did it the right way. In our model, the primary care physician was the captain of the ship who "managed" the patient's care. If a patient wanted to see a specialist, the primary care doctor had to approve it. Otherwise, the patient could walk into the orthopedist's or neurosurgeon's office just by making an appointment, which is extremely expensive and almost always causes duplication and waste. This stipulation brought a lot of resentment from

---

PAGE 6   ALABAMA HEALTH NEWS   SEPTEMBER 1988

ONE ON ONE

Henderson sees health care becoming centralized

"Ob/gyn? It's the most exciting, fulfilling field. I wouldn't want to do anything else. My work is so very rewarding and I look forward to it every day."

Ronald E. Henderson, M.D., was born in Prattville, attended the University of Alabama and went to medical school at the Medical College of Alabama. He did his internship and residency at University of Alabama Hospitals and Clinics.

While specializing in gynecology, obstetrics, and infertility, Henderson emphasizes preventive medicine and the long-term beneficial effects of a healthy lifestyle. He has been putting these prin-

present and it makes me think of the unique way the Chinese write the word "crisis". It's a combination of the two words "danger" and "opportunity". It's an opportunity for those willing to take risks.

AHN: HOW HAS THIS PARTICULAR SERVICE CHANGED THE MOST?

HENDERSON: It's incredibly different from when I started 20 years ago. We didn't have ultrasound, amniocentesis, fetal monitoring, sigmoidoscopy, except experimentally. It's a more comfortable

on call for obstetrical patients and we have plans for a third team. Also, we've enlarged our geographic service to Cullman, Sylacauga and Anniston for prenatal care and to see gynecology patients. Also, we have applied for national standards for health screenings and cancer screenings. If a patient is overweight, we suggest they see our nutritionist. If a patient is a smoker, we suggest they go to smoking cessation classes. We want to make this a one-stop shopping place. We offer primary care, specialty care and care for minor health problems.

And the most exciting thing about our

rather keep people from getting in trouble. Preventive medicine.

AHN: DO YOU BELIEVE MOST DOCTORS STRESS PREVENTIVE MEDICINE?

HENDERSON: Certainly not enough. For example, we have cardiovascular surgeons who put people through extensive, dangerous surgery and send them out without telling them what kind of diet they should be on. They don't always send them to a nutritionist for the very important information they need. There's inadequate follow-up with that surgeon regarding their patients.

And some doctors don't practice preventive medicine personally, and to me, that is very hypocritical. Approximately 30 percent of doctors still smoke. Now, for a physician to sit and smoke and tell his patients that smoking is an unhealthy thing to do, well, that's not being a very good role model. The same applies to the doctors who are obese. They tell their patients to lose weight. The way they look speaks louder than what they are saying and I think it affects their credibility. If they're going to set an example, let it be a

"BMC's costs far exceeded other hospitals we do business with. It seems to me their cost structure has gotten out of line."

Ron Henderson, M.D.
Founder, Chairman of the Board
Southeast Health Plan

The Prattville Progress, September 1988. *(see page 192 for full article)*

the specialist doctors. Eventually, we had to let go of the concept of the primary doctor managing the care because it was becoming an obstacle to our success.

In our model, we also created a "utilization committee" that looked at medical procedures and length of hospital stay to determine whether or not it was actually needed. We adopted AMA guidelines and set up subspecialty committees. Instead of us dictating to orthopedists how they should treat certain problems, we brought together an orthopedic subspecialty committee and let them create their own guidelines. Our belief was that we should not dictate to the doctor. We should not expect them to follow us unless they had some input.

Not all our changes were met with excitement. Once the guidelines were implemented, we caught some flack from doctors about certain restrictions. While I was seeing patients, George would field the irate phone calls. At that time, the standard hospital stay for a routine vaginal birth delivery was about five days. Our obstetrical subcommittee had determined the appropriate stay should be two days. George was like a marked man. He got the same question a hundred times, "Well, does Dr. Henderson follow these rules, too?" I helped make the rules and followed them religiously! People thought we were out of our minds. But we allowed three days if the patient had a C-section. If there were complications, if the patient were bleeding or had an issue such as an infection causing a fever, the stay could be extended. Our guidelines were not unreasonable, but it was a shocking change for the community to accept.

To create more efficiency in the system, we attempted to narrow the list of drugs from which a doctor could choose. We created a pharmacy therapeutics committee that included two deans of the schools of pharmacy in the state and representatives from the large pharmacy chains. For each therapeutic illness, we had a defined drug class and would list top drugs in terms of results. We wanted the doctors to know which drugs had the best effect for certain illnesses and how much they were going to cost. We were keeping budgets on each physician so that we could make peer-to-peer comparisons. When we put that out there, of course, our competitors made hay with it. The physicians took it very badly; they didn't like us putting any restrictions on them. They didn't want to have to open a book. It got so bad there for a month or two, George was afraid to go to the grocery store.

The doctors George encountered rarely wanted to talk about quality of care; it was more often about money. Reimbursement was a constant battle. George brought to the table not only his negotiating skill, but also, because he'd been in the hospital business, he could sit eyeball-to-eyeball and talk the game better than they could. But we always tried to be fair. One plastic surgeon who specialized in breast reductions and augmentations didn't think we were paying him enough. He got so mad at George that he sent him a large, thick envelope full of pictures of breasts, probably fifty pictures. He was trying to prove the value of the work he was doing, that it wasn't cosmetic but health-related. The fact is that breast reductions are necessary for those with back problems, as are augmentations for women following mastectomies. We ended up giving him what he wanted. Another such example was that sometimes a rhinoplasty is needed to correct a deviated septum. But a whole lot of people were coming out of surgery with beautiful noses billed to us as deviated septums. So we started asking for "before and after" pictures.

We learned a lot that we weren't expecting. The disparity in compensation between primary care and specialty care became clear and woke a lot of people up. But in the beginning, the attitude of our board was to always give the doctor the benefit of the doubt. As we got into it, we realized that although most medical professionals are trying to do the right thing, you've got a small group that creates a problem for everybody. All the rules and policies have to be made for them—everybody pays for the sins of a few.

We created a management committee to review claims exceeding $10,000 that were not hospital claims. Such a claim would be kicked out of the system and reviewed for appropriateness. If there was a claim we couldn't quite deal with ourselves, we could send it to a private review agency in California for an opinion on how much to pay. We had an orthopedic claim for a four-and-a-half-hour procedure to correct a curvature of the spine, including anesthesia time; but it was not a life-threatening procedure. The doctor's bill was $30,000. We sent that claim off to California. Their reply didn't suggest an appropriate payment; they just told us that we should report the doctor for fraud. We didn't want to barbeque any doctors, so we started trying to figure out what we should pay. Somebody said, "I think $1,000 an hour is a pretty good hourly rate. Let's send him a check for five grand, stamped 'Paid in Full,' and see what he does." You know what he did? Nothing. He took it. That's when we realized some doctors' attitude was, "If you don't catch me, that's your problem." With a typical indemnity insurance company and most of the health plans, that claim would hit the system electronically and process automatically; the doctor would get a check charged back to the employer, and no one would ever know about it.

We discovered all kinds of incredible things. We had constructed a database, that no one else in the industry had, that could compare physicians peer-to-peer. Today, gathering that data, manipulating it, and seeing the trends would not be a big deal. But back then, when emails and faxes didn't even exist, it was a huge advancement. When we conducted our comparisons, we learned that in internal medicine, as in all professions, there were a few bad apples. Some of the doctors with the most abusive practices were the most popular. The patient walks into the office and the doctor decides they're gonna get every test in the world, and the patient is thinking, "I'm getting *great* care." Patients didn't go to medical school, they have no way of knowing whether they need the tests or not; they trust their doctor. One of two things is usually happening here: either the physician is insecure in his ability to make judgments, so he's ruling out everything he can, or the physician is milking the system. Either he doesn't know what he's doing or he's building a new house. An uncertain or insecure doctor will drive you crazy with costs; they're very expensive doctors.

But this was also the heyday for lawyers to go after medical professionals. Defensive medicine had become the norm, and we understood that. If a doctor is being sued and is on the stand in a courtroom and some sharp lawyer asks, "Why didn't you run that test?" and the doctor says, "Well, I was trying to be frugal with the health-care dollar." That is not an acceptable answer in the courtroom. They'll roast you alive for that. It's been estimated that the legal system accounts for approximately thirty percent of the increase in health-care costs.

The hospitals didn't know how to take us at first, either. The leverage you have in this business is one, the volume of patients and two, the influence of our physician representation, on the board and actually participating. We had promised the providers that from the time we received a well-done claim form, we would turn around the cash within two weeks. And we held to that. We learned that you could get better arrangements with the hospitals and the physicians if you could get them their money quicker. Everybody else was sitting on the money. The hospitals loved it. We eventually had the support of all of the hospitals except for Montclair Baptist Medical Center. Montclair wanted to have their prices thirty percent higher than the other hospitals, which wouldn't have been fair. They basically wanted a commission from us to use the hospital. Therefore, we dropped Montclair Baptist as a provider. After that, two hospitals, on their own initiative, reduced their rates to us because they appreciated our stance.

DOCTOR'S CORNER

Ronald E. Henderson, M.D.

"From about the time I was in the tenth grade, I was focused on a career in medicine."

The minute you meet him, you know Dr. Ron Henderson loves his work. "I'm excited about what I do," he says. "I look forward to coming to work every day."

He says he owes much of his enthusiasm and accomplishments to a pair of powerful mentors from his boyhood in Prattville, Alabama. "Judge Livingston, who was the chief justice of the Alabama Supreme Court, often took me fox hunting with him when I was 12 or 13," says Dr. Henderson. "He inter-ested me in achieving all I could achieve."

Another mentor was Dr. George Newton, the family doctor in Prattville. "He took me along on his house calls when I was in my late teens," Dr. Henderson recalls. "From about the time I was in the tenth grade, I was focused on a career in medicine."

Dr. Henderson selected the obstetrics/gynecology specialty because it offered the opportunity for continuing care.

He wants the Henderson & Walton Women's Center to exert a positive influence on every patient. "I encourage everyone to live a balanced life. Five F's — family, friends, faith, fitness, finance — equal fun," he says. He follows his own advice — and makes one addition. "I try to do one new thing each year to keep the juices flowing," he says. "This year I'm learning to fly and working toward my private pilot's license."

Since Dr. Henderson began his practice in 1968, he says he's seen incredible changes in medicine. "Comparatively speaking, we were in the middle ages back then," he says, "and there are even more dramatic changes coming."

He anticipates an explosion of knowledge and technology — more organ replacements and artificial limbs in addition to the ability to make earlier diagnoses than are now possible. "There will be more emphasis on prevention in an effort to maintain quality health care while keeping costs down," he says.

Dr. Henderson is a graduate of the University of Alabama and the Medical College of Alabama. Upon completing his residency, he began practicing obstetrics and gynecology. He also is founder and chairman of the board of Southeast Health Plan. ∎

10

St. Vincent's publication, 1990.

The industry was very young, and there were no regulations in the state of Alabama to govern us. The state couldn't figure out what to do, so the Alabama Department of Insurance and the Alabama Department of Public Health decided they would both govern us. We were accountable to both departments, which was very frustrating since they didn't talk to each other. Working with the Department of Insurance attorneys, we actually helped draft the first laws for the state. We also formed the state's first HMO association, which all the others joined, and it became an oversight group for the entire state. We even got involved on a national level in Washington.

By the late 1980s, SEHP had become so successful that Blue Cross Blue Shield started to lowball us on premiums, undercutting us in Mobile, then Huntsville, then Montgomery, and then, lastly, Birmingham, because we were strongest in Birmingham. The state Department of Insurance kept increasing the amount of money we needed to have in reserve. I suspect that Blue Cross lobbyists were probably behind some of the increases. We never ran of money; we were forced to raise more capital only to meet those ever-increasing reserve requirements. Blue Cross was exempt from the reserve regulation; although by this point they had accumulated so much, it didn't matter. Then we started getting hit by the hospitals that would not accept our reimbursement for hospital stays. We were not trying to make a ton of money, we were trying to do what was best for the patient. In the process, we got all kinds of grief. The thing about it is, if they had supported us, *everybody* would have been better off. But it didn't work out that way.

In 1991, when the reserve requirements reached a certain level, we had to look for an investor. Billy Rushton, CEO of Protective Life, bailed us out. We sold Protective a piece of the company to raise capital for the reserves. They didn't need to put in a lot of money; just their presence kept the state Department of Insurance at bay. Billy Rushton retired in 1992, and a lawyer named Drayton Nabers came in as CEO of Protective. All Drayton cared about were the quarterly earnings for the life insurance.

Protective owned a big enough percentage of SEHP that their accountants required them to consolidate our numbers into theirs. We were in the midst of a database system change, converting the data so that our new system could read it, a complicated and expense process back then. We had had a very good year in 1990; in 1991, we had started the system change. For about a four-month period, we could not produce the data to support the numbers we were booking. We knew we were making money, but we just didn't have the data to back it up. At that time, Protective was consolidating our numbers, and their accountants, Coopers and Lybrand, got

CareNotes

Volume 7, No. 1   Spring 1991

Ronald E. Henderson, M.D.   Jeffrey Gunnells, M.D.
Philip D. Walton, M.D.   Carol G. Swindle, M.D.
Frank O. Page, M.D.   Berkeley S. Merrill, M.D.
John R. Faucette, M.D.   Cynthia L. Lassiter, M.D.
Charles Hudson, M.D.   Brenda C. Taylor, M.D.

STRESS FOR SUCCESS?

Whether in family life, finances or work, most of us want to achieve success. Too often, we begin to accept stress as a trade-off in the pursuit of success.

All of us at Henderson and Walton Women's Center are concerned about the amount of stress placed on women in today's society. Serving as the primary care physician for women, we see firsthand the toll that stress takes on the health of our patients.

Although it may seem impossible at times, *stress is manageable!* Listed below are some successful ways to handle stress:

- Make regular exercise a priority! Some type of cardiovascular (aerobic) exercise will help relieve *psychological* and *physical* stress.
- Aim for seven to eight hours of uninterrupted sleep per night. (This may vary with each individual.)
- Maintain a low-fat diet high in complex carbohydrates and adequate in protein.
- Select an occupation in which you find true enjoyment.
- Find time to relax, even if it is only ten minutes a day!
- Select hobbies/interests that you enjoy and that help you to "unwind."
- Nurture your love and affection for family members and friends through activities you enjoy. (i.e., baking bread, cross stitch, etc.)
- Develop close friendships with a few key women.
- Join a support group for particular challenges in your personal life.
- Plan a mini-vacation, even if it is only for one night or weekend.
- Set some goals. Even if it is just a few, achieving these goals will give you a good sense of accomplishment.

Dr. Henderson

A good balance can be obtained by examining your "wheel of life" supported by the five spokes of **faith, family, friends, fitness, and finance.** When of similar length, they will help your wheel to roll smoothly through life, thus leading to a less stressful, more enjoyable lifestyle.

All of the associates at Henderson and Walton Women's Center care about you and are interested in your health and happiness. As our physicians orchestrate your healthcare, one of our goals is to help you **be the best you can be!**

Dr. Ronald E. Henderson

HENDERSON&WALTON
WOMEN'S CENTER, P.C.

Top left, Beth and Ron, 1990. *Top right,* Ellen, Bill, and Rhonda, 1990. *Bottom,* St. Vincent's *Care Notes,* 1991.

very nervous because we couldn't produce that data. Coopers and Lybrand required us to increase our reserves, which threw us from profits to losses. It made it look like we were doing worse than we were doing and actually losing money. We knew we were cash flow positive but could not prove it.

Drayton was assuming the helm of Protective, and he didn't want any division losing money. And it looked to him like we were losing money. Of all the lines of business that Protective was involved in, health care was probably the most volatile. No matter how well you manage health care, you can never prevent accidents or pancreatic cancer. It's just the nature of the business; you're going to have good and bad years. Our industry was more volatile than he really wanted to accept.

Late one night, Drayton, George, and I had a come-to-Jesus meeting, and Drayton decided to sell Protective's percentage of our company, which was significant. We didn't want him to sell to an industry player, but he didn't really care; he just wanted out. He and George made a deal that Drayton would look for a buyer in the industry, and we'd try to raise money from the venture capitalist world, and whoever offered the best price would get the Protective shares. We had so many damn things working against us at one time—we had to let it go. We ended up finding a group of investors with a solid offer to buy the entire company. The deal resulted in a good return for Protective; they had tripled their money in very little time, less than a year and a half.

Southeast Health Plan was a great company—we had a great board, a great team, and very committed people. Our board meetings were well run; there was no jockeying for position. Everybody was just trying to do the right thing. We had representation all over the city. Over the eleven-year span of the company's existence, we learned a lot. Making the transition from the provider to the payer, for all of us, was a gigantic leap. It is a very different way of looking at health care. We had more than five hundred doctors as investors, and they all made money. When it all spun out, I made more money because I had more invested. It wasn't a home run, but it wasn't a loser. We had kept the patient as the center of focus, and I slept soundly at night.

In 1993, the venture capitalists sold the company again, and it was absorbed by the Physicians Corporation of America (PCA) based in Miami. PCA, at the same time they were buying us, were selling themselves to Humana. By buying us and another company, they were increasing their valuation, and they were successful.

Today, with the requirements and the regulatory demands, it would be much more expensive and very difficult to start an HMO based on our model. Kaiser Permanente in California has done it right. They take care of their patients and still pay a dividend. They are vertically integrated and control it all; they own the hospital, and all the doctors all work for them. Kaiser is probably the best that we've ever seen in this industry.

I would do it all over again, even knowing the outcome. Because of our efforts, Blue Cross Blue Shield of Alabama began using some of the same approaches to reimbursing for medical care. They actually started a "Preferred Provider" program, and I was one of three consultants that advised them on the design of the program, which still exists today.

AVIATION AND THE 5552XRAY

In the early days of Southeast Health Plan, I had a phenomenal experience concerning aviation. Dr. Richard "Dick" McLaughlin, the medical director for SEHP, was a pilot and owned a small plane. One summer, my family was at the beach for our annual weeklong vacation, and I had board responsibilities back in Birmingham. Dick volunteered to fly me to the beach to be with my family and then graciously flew back, picked me up, and brought me back to Birmingham. That changed my whole life for the next twenty years and made me a lifelong aviation enthusiast.

At the Birmingham airport, Dr. Evan Zeiger Sr. was running a Fixed Base Operator (FBO), a service station for airplane operators, and offered an aviation course. I took ground school for one year and then started training for my private license. I got tired of going from plane to plane and having to relearn all the bells and whistles. I bought a fixed-gear Cherokee Six, a type of airplane that cruised at 140 knots, which I named "600 Bravo Hotel" after my wife, Beth Henderson (300 was already taken). My teacher was Mark Gilman, a real laid-back, easygoing young man about twenty-five years of age. I would leave my office at 5:30 p.m. and meet Mark to take my lessons in the air. The first stage of lessons was in the fall, and I can still remember turning into the western sun and having to learn to deal with it and maintain altitude. It was extremely exciting and rewarding. I was hooked.

DEPARTMENT OF TRANSPORTATION

FEDERAL AVIATION ADMINISTRATION

Pilot Proficiency Award Program
This is to certify that
Ronald E. Henderson

has satisfactorily completed the requirements to become eligible to wear
the Pilot Proficiency Wings, Phase **II** attesting to this
individual's dedication to aviation safety.

A. B. Ashbury
A. B. Ashbury
MANAGER, RAL FSDO
Signature

February 7, 1998
Date

Top left, The Cherokee, 1989.
Top right, Ron and grandson
Matthew, gearing up for takeoff
in the Cherokee, 1996. Bottom,
Pilot Certification, 1988.

After receiving my instrument and commercial ratings, I bought a brand-new Bonanza T-Tail in 1990, not to be confused with the Bonanza V-Tail, known as the "doctor killer." This plane—with the number "5552XRAY" on the outside, which I also used as my call number when communicating with the towers—continued to be my ride for the next twenty-four-hundred hours of flight time and exciting aviation experiences. It absolutely shrunk the globe and gave me a much longer reach for my entrepreneurial activities. I flew this plane all over the eastern United States from 1A9-Prattville, to BHM-Birmingham and as far as Gardner, Colorado, right at the base of the Rocky Mountains. For my Twin Valley Farms' Angus operation, I flew from 1A9-Prattville all over the Southeast and as far west as southwestern Kansas. I remember returning from a cattle sale in southwestern Kansas with my son Bill, cruising twelve-thousand feet above the land at a speed of 240 knots per hour. That was very exciting! I flew several times to south Florida to market Twin Valley Farms, LLC, and to purchase high-grade genetic Angus cattle.

Beth did not take great joy in flying in our small plane. One time, Beth and I were going to fly our plane to Gardner, Oklahoma, to visit our friends, the Bittners. There were some weather issues, but I looked at the radar and showed Beth how we could fly around the edge of the storms. "I don't want to do that," she said. Finally, the weather got good enough, and I insisted that we take off. We were flying at twelve-thousand feet and the wind had caused us to "crab," so that we had to counter the wind. Beth saw a sharp spike on the storm scope. She said, "What's that?" I said, "It's lightning in the panhandle of Texas, but we're not going that way." Then she saw another, and then another, and suddenly five or six spikes. It was a thunderstorm in the panhandle of Texas. "I want to land," she said, very emphatically. So we landed in Liberal, Kansas, and borrowed the little airport's one car, one of the original Hondas, to drive to a local motel. That night, I slept on my side of the bed, mad, and she slept on her side of the bed, mad. The next morning we had to get up and find somewhere to eat, which wasn't easy. As we took off, there was a small sandstorm in front of our plane. She said, "What's that?" I ignored her!

MEDISPHERE, 1992–1997

During the early '90s, Clinton had just been elected president and Hilary was going to roll out her new health-care plan; in anticipation of this, the industry was consolidating. The consensus at this time was that physicians should unify and take advantage of economies of scale to be in control of their own destiny, mainly to prevent a government takeover of health care. Practices all over the country were merging, most of them multi-specialty and a few single-specialty.

For years, it had been like a "Parade of Homes" at Henderson & Walton because physicians from across the Southeast, and one from Maryland, came to see the infrastructure of our practice. They were very impressed with our business model, which provided for the lowest expenses relative to revenue of any practice in the region. Our accountant, Belinda Cornelius, was spending a lot of her time showing people around. I saw it as an exceptional opportunity to build a practice management company. I named it MediSphere because it spoke to medicine and to a large size company.

We started working on MediSphere in early 1991. Our practice management model was to convince ob-gyn practices to merge and allow us to oversee the business side of their practices. We brought in Warren Smedley, the husband of Rhonda's best friend at Vanderbilt, from New York as our vice president of marketing. I asked Belinda to handle the controller work and take care of all accounting issues. We went to see our accountant, Paul Kassouf, to explain the concept to him. One of the accountants on Paul's staff, Wes Brown, started researching ways to handle the equity and practice management companies.

By late 1991, we had gotten MediSphere organized and were in the process of raising the capital. We made a conscious decision that we were not going to bring in venture capital money. The firm we were competing against in Birmingham, MedPartners, had brought in several million dollars' worth of venture money. They basically sold sixty percent of their company to a venture firm that provided startup capital. We just didn't want to do that; we were trying to stay doctor-owned.

In 1992, we hired Wes Brown away from Kassouf to come work as Medi Sphere's chief financial officer. We knew what we wanted to do, and he fit right into our plan, our first choice. It was a gutsy move, Wes moving from an established firm over to this fledgling company. At first, Belinda and Wes shared a tiny little office at the end the hall next to my office. The

Ron Henderson, doctor and cattleman
Fields of care

Nothing is halfway with Ron Henderson, '59, MD '62. And it never has been. Growing up on a rural cotton, corn and cattle farm in the '40s and '50s in Prattville, Ala., Ronald E. Henderson was introduced to a strict work ethic at a very early age. His parents saw to it that he gave an effort of 100 percent in everything he did, especially his cotton-picking and corn-gathering chores. At age 55 Henderson still abides by that labor-intense ethic. Those old-fashioned, nose-to-the-grindstone principles, say friends, got Henderson where he is today.

The founder, president and chief executive officer of Henderson & Walton Women's Center in Birmingham, Henderson has become one of the most respected physicians in the country. And, as the owner of Twin Valley Farms in Prattville, he is also one of the nation's most successful Angus beef cattle breeders.

"I am the luckiest guy in the world," Henderson says. "My work is my hobby. I love medicine. I love people. And I also have this incredible love for agriculture, particularly cattle."

For more than 20 years, Henderson has been a leader in making quality medical care accessible to women in and around the Birmingham area. While specializing in gynecology, obstetrics and infertility, Henderson emphasizes preventive medicine and the long-term beneficial effects of a healthy lifestyle. Based at St. Vincent's Hospital, Henderson & Walton Women's Center is one of the largest private practices of its kind in the country. The practice also has six satellite offices in cities surrounding Birmingham—Alabaster, Anniston, Cullman, Jasper, Sylacauga and Tuscaloosa, and a center is scheduled to open in Atlanta in 1993.

Even while building a prominent medical practice, Dr. Ron Henderson has not lost touch with his rural roots, as he also operates the successful Twin Valley Farms in Prattville.

43 **Joseph Allen Lee**, LLB '50, retired in October as attorney for the City of Scottsboro, Ala., after 36 years of service. He will continue to work in private practice.

50 The American Society of Civil Engineers presented a certificate of appreciation to **Charlie H. Cook** of Montgomery, Ala., during its annual convention Aug. 14 at Gulf Shores, Ala.

After retiring from McDonnell Douglas Corporation in 1986, **George Shirley Mills** helped form Heritage Music On Video Inc., a non-profit corporation that travels around the country to videotape organized jazz festivals. Anyone wishing more information on the corporation may contact Mills at (314) 822-1005.

A.T. "Tim" Wuska, technical director of ACIPCO, retired in July after 42 years of service. He lives in Vestavia Hills, Ala.

51 **Lewis W. Gamble** of Greenville, S.C., has retired as marketing sales and service specialist for Monsanto Textiles Company.

State Farm Insurance Company regional vice president **Robert W. Hodgkins** retired in July. Friends and associates at State Farm have established a Robert W. Hodgkins Endowed Scholarship in the College of Commerce in honor of his retirement.

53 Harwick Chemical vice president and Board of Directors member **George H. Proodian** has retired after 30 years of service. He lives in Akron, Ohio.

54 **Ralph O. McGee**, of Point Clear, Ala., has retired from his position as international relief captain on the Boeing 747-200.

59 The Board of Directors of Westinghouse Electric Corporation has elected **Emmett B. Wheeler Jr.** vice president of the corporation.

60 Kappa Delta has honored **Mary Winston McCall Laseter**, MA '78, of Tuscaloosa with the Order of the Emerald.

62 The Maryland Psychological Association has elected **Carolyn Calhoun Battle** to the position of president for 1993-94.

63 **Robert A. Culp Jr.**, MA '65, PhD '67, has been named director of purchasing and traffic for Ashland Petro-

Alabama Alumni, University of Alabama magazine, December 1992. *(continued on page 193)*

office was so small, their chairs touched back-to-back, and they'd have to say, "Could you move over? I need to get up." I would typically see patients until 5:30 or 6 p.m., and they knew not to bother me when I was seeing patients. But they might be able to catch me after my post-lunch power nap or if I went near my office, if they lay in wait.

Belinda had created an extremely accurate accounting of what we were doing at Henderson & Walton. It was easy to take what we had built—departments like purchasing and marketing, and move some staff to MediSphere. The systems were already there in embryonic stages. Nan Priest, who had been in charge of managed care for Southeast Health Plan, moved over to navigate the insurance side of the business. She was dynamite. We moved Dee Park over to help with the marketing.

We also brought my son, Bill, onboard as senior vice president of development. Bill traveled the country recruiting doctors for MediSphere. Our pitch was that our practice management model had the lowest expenses relative to revenue of any practice we'd seen. That was the selling point, and people were looking for it. They knew changes were coming.

Toward the end of the year, we had everything organized and started approaching practice groups. We spread out to cover more territory, and in the first couple of years we probably hit a hundred ob-gyn groups in Alabama, Mississippi, and Georgia. MedPartners of Birmingham was going after multi- and single-specialty practices, so they started competing against us in Atlanta for ob-gyns. At the time, we were talking to probably fifteen ob-gyn groups in Atlanta. One night we had a big showdown. Our group made our presentation on a stage at Piedmont Hospital in the Buckhead area of Atlanta. As we were walking out, the competition came walking in, and we stared them down as we passed by.

Our first ob-gyn merger was with a group at Northside Hospital in Atlanta, which at the time was the largest baby hospital in the country, averaging ten thousand deliveries a year. Soon after we got them to join, we opened another office in Gwinnett County, near I-85, the fastest growing area in the country. Every time you'd go through there, it seemed they had added another lane to the interstate. Once we got the Northside Hospital and the Gwinnet office up and running, then we really began to generate more interest. We even got a couple of groups in Birmingham to join us, including a pediatric group.

Our small staff of five people were all in their twenties, and I called them "the executives." They just knocked themselves out every single day. We

TWIN VALLEY

Twin Valley Farms' owner Dr. Ron Henderson

Agriculture and Medicine

THE PERFECT ROMANCE

BY MARK MORRISON

Nothing is halfway with Ron Henderson. And it never has been. Growing up on an Autauga County cotton, corn and cattle farm in the '40s and '50s, he was introduced at a very early age to a dedicated work ethic that was labor intense. His parents saw to it that he gave an effort of 100 percent in everything he did, especially his cotton-picking and corn-gathering chores.

At 55, Dr. Ron Henderson still abides by the strong work ethic he learned as a youngster. It is those old-fashioned, nose-to-the-grindstone principles, say friends, that got Henderson where he is today.

The owner of Twin Valley Farms in Prattville, Henderson is one of the most successful Angus beef cattle breeders in the country. And, as the founder, president and chief executive officer of Henderson & Walton Women's Center in Birming-

ham, he is also one of the nation's most respected physicians.

"I am the luckiest guy in the world," says Henderson. "My work is my hobby. I love medicine. I love people. And I also have this incredible love for agriculture, particularly cattle."

In 1991, Twin Valley Farms, which covers more than 1,800 acres, registered 286 Angus beef cattle with the American Angus Association—the most by any Alabama Angus breeder. By the end of calving season in May 1993, Henderson plans to have more than 300 registered Angus. According to American Angus Association officials in Missouri, Twin Valley Farms has one of the largest operations in the Southeast. Of the national organization's 12,418 members who registered Angus beef cattle last year, there were only 23 herds that registered 300 head or more. Twin Valley ranked 30th last year as far as annual registrations, officials said.

As for his medical practice, Henderson has been a leader in making quality medical care accessible to women in and around the Birmingham area for more than 20 years. While specializing in gynecology, obstetrics and infertility, Henderson emphasizes preventive medicine and the long-term beneficial effects of a healthy

16

Neighbors, Alfa magazine, October 1992. (continued on page 194)

would travel and arrive at our prospect's site before daylight and leave after dark. The staff would even pull their own wires for computers. Our biggest challenge was to convince the doctors to give up control. It's very hard to approach physicians who have built their own practices from the ground up and tell them, "We're going to take the business decision-making away from you. You just practice medicine, and we'll manage the operations." Doctors are not known for their business acumen, and this transition most often improves the quality of their professional and personal lives. Wes and Belinda—now at Kassouf—are still doing this. It's a solid concept—you know you're going to make the doctors' lives better, make them "smile more and earn more."

The plane was an incredible tool that allowed us to work all day in the office, fly to a distant meeting, and come home to sleep in our own beds. One night after a meeting, we took off from the small Charlie Brown Field airport just outside Atlanta. I'd seen the pilot report: "icing at six thousand feet." Warren was in the front seat and Dee and Belinda in the back. At about four thousand feet, Warren said, "REH, we've got a beautiful something on the wing, it looks like ice!" The plane didn't have any heat on the wings. I had just gotten back from a four-day pilot's course in Orlando that covered icing, and I knew in that situation, you just can't keep going, you must put the nose down and land. I radioed the tower and learned that the nearest airport was in Carrolton, Georgia. We positioned ourselves right toward it, left downwind, on runway 36. When we got below the freezing level, the plane suddenly shook, wrenching back and forth. In the back, they were quietly praying.

As we skimmed in just above the southern pines, with the plane rocking, we met with a crosswind, which wasn't a problem, but it scared my passengers even more. Dee was crying and praying. We had to go under the radar by a mountain, so nobody knew where we were, and we didn't know where the mountain was. Finally, we got down low enough to the ground and started leveling out. We landed with Dee still crying and Warren an absolute wreck. I told them, "You just can't buy experience like this." Dee never got back on the plane. Beth later said, "Ron, that is cruel making people who don't like to fly get on a plane. They have families! You say, 'Come on, let's fly to the meeting,' and they can't say no to you!" From then on, I tried not to put the more hesitant staff on the spot about flying with me.

At one point, MediSphere had a big deal going on in Indianapolis, Indiana, and we also needed to close some deals in Raleigh, North Carolina. Wes and I flew to Raleigh and did our wrap-up thing there. And then we were going to make a cross-country flight over the mountains into Indiana.

As Wes crawled into the cockpit, I handed him his plastic milk jug. He said, "What is this?" And I said, "It's your bathroom." It was a three-hour flight, and we weren't going to make any stops. At that time, the US military was designing the Stealth aircraft fighter planes. I had filed our flight plan, and we had just gotten airborne from Raleigh when I said to Wes, "You're going to really like this…" About a minute later, we saw what looked like mosquitos way out in the distance, and about thirty seconds later a squadron of those brand-new fighters, which nobody had ever seen before, came flying right over us. What a tremendous sensation.

We had two guys on our legal team who had never flown before, and they kept asking when they were going to get to fly. So we took them with us on our trip to Columbus, Mississippi, to meet with an internal medicine group. There were six of us in the plane, and as we taxied out on the runway, we were all chatting. One lawyer, Scott Russell, was in the front seat—it was his first flight and he was all excited. As we're scooting down the runway, I realized right away that we were not going fast enough. I radio the tower that we were going to abort takeoff, and everyone went very quiet. As we drove back to the hanger, I explained to the staff that we couldn't get enough speed but that I didn't know what was going on. We were almost to the hanger when this guy walked out and looked at the plane, wide-eyed, and began to gesture. He ran back into the hanger and back out with a fire extinguisher. Apparently, the left wheelbase was on fire. Steve Johnson, the other attorney,

Ron and grandson Matthew, with the plane 5552XRAY at airport in Prattville, 1998.

asked, "Isn't the left wheel base over the fuel?" Once he said that, the whole group began to pile out. For some reason, Scott was still sitting there in the front seat, and I had to say, "Scott, you need to get moving."

By 1993, our practice management company was going great guns, with eighty-five doctors in five states. Resisting venture capital money had been easy through our first few acquisitions, but we just didn't have enough capital to keep functioning without it. We had pushed the banks about as far as we could to borrow their money. We next brought in a small investment group, Jemison Investment from Birmingham, who put in some money. But we needed substantial capital to keep purchasing assets, paying staff, and traveling to all these sites. We had a team of development people who just traveled around trying to find groups for us to approach. Once we got past our third or fourth acquisition, we'd run our capital about as far as we could run it, even with the Birmingham investors.

On top of our lack of capital, I was feeling fatigued and even weakened. We had made friends with a venture firm in New York, but we couldn't agree on terms. But they helped us find a CEO-type who could take over for me. Fred Fink had worked for a big consulting group out of San Francisco, and had set up major operations including Mayo Clinic in Rochester, Minnesota, and Cleveland Clinic. He was very smart and knew what he was doing. I remained chairman of the board. Fred came to Birmingham and for nine months he lived at our house, in Bill's old room. Beth remembers me saying, "Oh, you can stay with us!" Although he had promised to move to Birmingham, I think Fred had planned to move the headquarters to New York. But I'd go to bed with Fred and get up with Fred. I'd work all day seeing patients, come home, eat, and stay up talking to Fred until 11 p.m., night after night. And Beth would tell me, "You're under stress and overdoing it." And I would say, "No I'm not, I'm having fun."

By 1992, I was practicing four days a week as well as serving as chairman of the board of Southeast Health Plan. As the CEO of MediSphere, I was traveling all over the Southeast to visit our members and beyond to see prospects. Suddenly, I was having three to four meetings a week and was getting home after 11 p.m., only to begin practice again the next morning at 6 a.m. I was having a great time; but Beth kept warning me that although I did not feel any stress, I had to be under tremendous strain. I didn't give it much thought; I just kept pushing.

The MediSphere pace was 24/7. We were all working long hours, traveling all over to manage the practices that we had purchased, and visiting prospects. We were still closing deals—we didn't have any money, but we were still closing deals. Fred got Belinda, Wes, and me in front of some really receptive venture groups in New York. The first firm we approached was on Wall Street, on the fifty-fourth floor of a skyscraper. We walked in to meet the three venture capitalists and were confronted with a long, glass table supported by sculpted women's legs on ballet point. Belinda was distracted the whole meeting. Another time, Wes and Fred flew up and were picked up by a black limo, Wes's first, that took them across the bridge to Connecticut, to a building next to a little startup company called ESPN. This group of venture capitalist understood our business better than others, but we couldn't get beyond the feeling that we were lying to our existing shareholders about diluting the company with non-physician ownership. So eventually Fred had to move on.

We got word that HealthSouth had just bought a company called Surgical Care Affiliates (SCA). The chief operating officer of SCA, Bill Hamburg, made $80 million in the deal and was looking for his next venture. He'd gotten some money from two New York investment firms and put together a team of bright people. Wes and I flew my plane to Nashville to meet with Bill in the airport. This was Wes's first experience with wind shear. He was seated in the front of the plane next to me and heard the tower give us a wind shear warning as we were coming in for a landing. They barely got it out of their mouths when we dropped fifty feet. It's like hitting a brick wall in the air. We got off the plane, and Wes was a little sea sick. The meeting started, and he hardly knew what anybody was saying because he was trying to figure out how he could rent a car and drive back to Birmingham.

We had learned to trust our first impressions, and on meeting Bill we both had an instant positive reaction. He had on cowboy boots and an ankle-length black jacket, the fashion in Nashville at the time. Casual clothes, laid-back guy. We talked health-care numbers and walked out of there real impressed with him. Bill told me, "If I do this, Ron, I want you to stay on as chairman of the board. We need your physician input." We came back to Birmingham and talked with Belinda, Dee, Warren, and Nan, the executive group. Everybody but Nan wanted to go forward. Everybody else understood that we needed money.

Bill Hamburg was going to buy our company and assume all our bank debt, lock, stock, and barrel. We felt a heavy responsibility; all our customers had committed themselves to our vision and decision-making. We began to clandestinely supply a ton of data to Nashville. We had to wait until the fifty people working in our office went home for the day to use the fax machines, feeding single sheets into those early, slow machines. On one level, it felt like we were selling out our customers. But we needed money because we had a pipeline full of people wanting to join. I could sell it and they would buy it, but we didn't have the money to pay for it. It was a painful experience.

Eventually, we closed the deal. Nan moved on from MediSphere, but everybody else stayed. My son Bill continued in his development role until 1999. Warren stayed on for a little while longer. Wes moved to Nashville as part of the deal. And there were two guys up there who didn't appreciate him coming in on top, so he had some politics to deal with. Once all the logistics were handled, it didn't take long to push full steam ahead, not when you've got $20 million of fresh capital. Bill Hamburg hired Cynthia Dotson as chief financial officer; she was very smart, a little manipulative, but she knew her numbers. If the development people would line it up, she and Wes would meet their accounting and legal team and close the deal while sitting there. At one point, MediSphere was in fourteen states and had almost two hundred physicians.

At that point we had no competition in ob-gyn. We moved quickly into Colorado, and had rapid activity in Arkansas. With this kind of momentum, we actually became profitable, with free cash flow, no debt, and money in the bank. Then the two big guys in the practice management industry, MedPartners and PhyCor, began bidding against each other for each sale. If a prospect was worth $10 million, the bidding war would drive the price up to $18 million. They were way overpaying. Wall Street said, *Unless the two of y'all merge, we're never going to get our money back out of this business.* So the two companies went through about six months of due diligence to merge. Bill Hamburg and I were on the plane coming back from California after meeting with doctors in Walnut Grove when we heard the news. And I said, "Oh, my God, the whole culture has changed."

About that time, I had become increasingly overwhelmed and exhausted. I decided to retire from the board. Belinda had decided to move on to work directly for St. Vincent's. Wes looked up and everybody he knew was gone; he saw the writing on the wall and took a job with PhyCor. The investors eventually sold off different parts of MediSphere. Henderson & Walton stayed with them until 2001. Wall Street had finally said, *We're not interested in this industry anymore because of the inflated prices.* Nobody could get their money back out of a purchase. It tanked quickly. The physicians knew what was going on and did not hold us responsible, didn't feel like we had done them wrong. A lot of our doctors called me to check on my health and see how I was doing. They would add, "We know it's a tough environment out there, and we understand," even though they had been hurt financially.

THOSE ALL-IMPORTANT CHURCHILL MORNINGS

In the early years, my staff dreaded Monday mornings because all weekend long I'd been reading and learning about new health-care, political, and business trends. I'd spend the mornings propped up in bed at the farm, reading until noon; Beth would even bring me my shredded wheat. I called these "Churchill mornings" because Winston Churchill used to read all the national newspapers and his mail in bed, dictating to secretaries. Information is power—those who get in first do the best. The following Monday mornings in staff meetings, I'd start talking about implementing these new ideas, and I could see the fear in their eyes. My staff would say, "We don't know if we can do this…" And I'd say, "Well, that's where health care is going. Don't look at me like a calf looks at a new fence!"

One weekend, I read about "directed care," an insurance product that strengthened the position of physicians. I briefly covered the basics for my five executives, and I could see they were rattled. They responded with, "We have no idea what you're talking about. There is no way it's going to work." But I knew how intelligent and competent they were, that they would figure it out. I told them that we were going to talk to the Lee family, owners of Buffalo Rock Beverage Company, and sell them on the directed care program. In no time at all, Warren and Wes were sitting in front of Mr. James C. Lee III saying, "directed care-this, and directed care-that." Mr. Lee asked, "Do you have the physician network to support it?" And Wes said, "No, but we'll have one by the time we need it." You just can't think about what you *can't* do.

In all my endeavors, I surrounded myself with winners—my staff just knocked themselves out. I believe I was intuitive when hiring people. I know some of my interviewing techniques pushed the boundaries, such as my questions on gun control, which offered insight into a candidate's thinking. More importantly, though, I've been told that I was able to motivate the people around me to achieve things they never thought they could achieve. After I'd given staff their Monday morning challenge or "do-list" a few times, they wanted to be able to do it. And they knew that if they didn't get it done, I was going to ask why not. I pushed them out of the nest a few times, which is the way you grow. After a while, they didn't think twice about it; they'd think, *Here's my list; it didn't kill me before, so it most likely won't kill me this time.* They just got it done.

My staff knew I was committed to the core, and they picked up on the energy and the vision and made it happen. When times got tough I'd tell 'em, "You can't buy this kind of experience." While I tried to always know when to call it quits if something just wasn't working, if I felt like we were moving in the right direction, I'd keep on pushing. I tried to teach them to not be afraid of failure, to be risk takers. If we fail, don't look back and piss and moan. It just didn't work.

Prayer of the Grandfather To Be

Our Dear Heavenly Father,

Thank you for my mother and father and all they gave to me. Thank you for my ancestors before them and what they caused me to be. Thank you for my wonderful wife and the world she has allowed me to see. Thank you for my daughters — oh, how they have blessed and taught me. Thank you for my son and all that he means to me. Thank you for my son-in-law and the many ways he has enhanced his wife's happiness. Thank you for his family and forebears and their contribution to the special one.

Now be with my daughter as she carries my grandson. Keep her safe and healthy, strong and aware of how really blessed we are. Give her her mother's kind and compassionate ways as she becomes a mother herself. Allow her the spiritual awareness to appreciate the complete meaning of this most special of events.

Be with my grandson during his dangerous but exciting voyage, as he moves from his current dependent existence to a more independent and autonomous life. Make him healthy, energetic, intelligent, and strong, but also giving, loving, and compassionate. Give his family the patience and wisdom to mold and develop him to his full potential. Give me the wisdom to be the role model I need and want to be.

Now, thank you for all the blessings sent my way. I consider myself only somewhat worthy, but am sincerely appreciative to have been so divinely blessed.

In Jesus Christ's name I pray, **Amen**

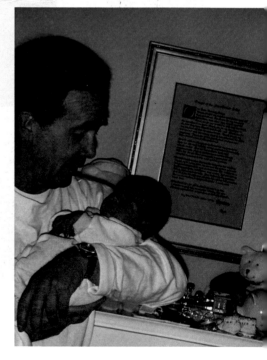

Above, Prayer of the Grandfather to Be, written by Ron for his first grandchild, Matthew. Right, "Papa" Ron and newborn grandson Matthew Powell, 1994.

CHAPTER 9

THE MYASTHENIA GRAVIS EXPERIENCE

1994–2003

Our first grandchild, Matthew Thomas "Papa's Boy" Powell, was born on January 10, 1994, in Jackson, Mississippi. That spring, I had a short spell of weakness and fatigue. I blew this off as a "valley-after-mountain" experience following the high from the birth of our first grand-child. By July of that year, the symptoms had become much worse. I got to the point that I had to have a senior colleague scrub in with me and do most of the surgery because of the weakness and fatigue. On September 30, 1994, I retired from practice completely. This was a necessary but excruciatingly painful decision. I continued at the helm of MediSphere, traveling to meetings and making presentations. In the summer of 1995, I was in a meeting and my head suddenly fell backward. Amazingly, no one noticed, and I finished the meeting by cupping my hands underneath my chin to support my head, leaning forward intently to listen and talk.

The symptoms continued to get worse, and I made a terrible mistake that all physicians are warned against—I self-diagnosed my illness as amyotrophic lateral sclerosis, ALS, or Lou Gehrig's disease. ALS is a much dreaded, always fatal neurological disease in which the voluntary muscles of the body waste away rapidly because of an attack on the nerve cells that control these muscles. Most patients die within three to five years of diagnosis. I had many of the symptoms, including problems with my grip, loss of muscle strength, muscle twitching, and extreme fatigue. I planned to work as long as I could, short of practicing medicine. One weekend, Beth was already visiting our new grandson in Jackson, and I was flying my plane, accompanied by my son Bill, to join them. I confided in him that I thought I had ALS, and he responded by putting his hand on my shoulder and saying, "Dad, don't worry—we'll get through it together, just as we always have." I will never forget the overwhelming emotion of that moment.

ALS is a uniformly fatal, horrible death. We didn't have the Internet back then, so I spent a lot of hours in the medical libraries reading the current scientific literature, checking my symptoms against different diagnoses. I knew a lot about them. When I determined that I had ALS, I went to my dear friend and rheumatologist, Dr. Bill Dodson. I said to him, "Bill, I have ALS and I would like for you to be my doctor." He said, "Ron, I can't do it, you're too much of a friend." I respected him for making that decision.

In November of 1995, I had flown my plane to North Carolina for Medi-Sphere business and back, arriving home after dark. Beth had cooked steaks for dinner, and in chewing the steak, I ran into problems. I simply could not chew efficiently, which I recognized as a new symptom—weakness in my muscle of mastication or chewing. Right there at the table I said, "Beth, good news and bad news. Good news is I don't have ALS, bad news is I have myasthenia gravis." Myasthenia gravis (MG) is a rare, chronic, neuromuscular autoimmune disease that causes profound muscle weakness and an all-consuming fatigue. ALS patients lose their ability to swallow first and then their ability to chew. I could still swallow, so I deduced it must be myasthenia gravis.

I went to see a respected neurologist and close friend, Dr. David O'Neal. He ordered two hours of testing on me, which included the diagnostic test using the chemical Tensilon, to which I had a positive response. After working me up, he confirmed the diagnosis of myasthenia gravis. Dr. O'Neal started me on Mestinon, the first-line drug therapy for the disease, at the highest dose recommended, and I improved somewhat.

For general health-care management, I continued to see my friend and pulmonologist, Dr. J. Terrell Spencer. In February of 1996, Dr. O'Neal asked that I see his UAB colleague, Dr. Shin Oh, an international expert on myasthenia gravis. Dr. Oh strongly recommended that I add immunosuppressive drug therapy to my treatment regime. He suggested adding 60 mg of prednisone and 200 mg of Imuran daily. I resisted, knowing that there were long-term risks associated with immunosuppressants. I knew that prednisone, a steroid medication, could put you at risk for osteoporosis, diabetes, cataracts, and glaucoma. And on a day-to-day basis, prednisone can cause side effects that make you jittery, interfere with your sleeping

Top left, Ron, Beth, and Matthew before a 1995 annual "Breeding Age Bull Sale" at TVF. *Top right,* Beth and Ron at 1995 sale. *Bottom,* Top seller breeding age bull, $4,000.

pattern, cause mood swings, and increase your vulnerability to infections. Imuran, meanwhile, carries long-term risks for certain cancers. I ended up taking 200 mg of Imuran and 60 mg of prednisone daily for five years.

Those years were very difficult. In the beginning, Beth and I spent most of our time at our Twin Valley Farms home in Prattville, rather secluded from most of our relatives and all our friends. I did a lot of strange things. I was up by four o'clock every morning. I called the contractor building our tennis courts around 5 a.m. and asked him what he was going to do that day. For a period of time, I was so weak that Beth had to help me dress. Our children did not like this secluded arrangement, so after several months we returned to Birmingham.

I became reclusive as well as secretive about my condition. Being disabled, having to always depend on someone else, brought on a serious depression. Although I was on an antidepressant drug, I remained below baseline emotionally. I began to have very personal conversations with God and prayed that *His will be done*. I also decided that if I was not going to get better, then I was ready to leave this world. These prayers began to have a very comforting effect on me both physically and emotionally, and my depression lifted. Years later, when I described these low points to my best lifelong friend from Prattville, Joe Chambliss, he teared up and was hurt that I hadn't told him I was so seriously ill.

Angus Spirit
10th Annual Production Sale

Noon
Saturday, April 8, 1995

At the farm near
Prattville, Alabama

Top left, Twin Valley Farms sale catalogue, 1995. *Top right,* Aerial photo of
Twin Valley Farms, 1995. *Bottom left,* Henderson family gathered for the 1995
Angus Spirit cattle sale. Front, from left: Lyn holding Lauren, Beth, and Rhonda.
Back: Bill, Ellen, Ron, and Tommy. *Bottom right,* Ron and Lauren, 1995.

FIGHTING MY WAY BACK

I went as crazy as a yo-yo on the steroids—couldn't sleep at all, and my face was swollen like a balloon. After five years of struggle, I called Dr. Oh and asked him how to get off of the immunosuppressants. He said, "Ron, I would rather you not get off the Imuran and prednisone." I replied, "Dr. Oh, I did not call you to ask you if I *could* get off those drugs, I am asking you *how* to get off the drugs." He held his position until the next day when he called back and said, "Ron, I think you should decrease them gradually over a period of several months. Please call me if you have any difficulty in doing so." I thanked him profusely and immediately began decreasing my dosage.

After a period of about six months, I was off the Imuran completely and began reducing the dosage of prednisone. I started a very mild exercise program, walking outside with a cane constructed with a fold-down seat that allowed me to sit and take a rest. Each day, I would go downstairs to my computer to do my praying, and then I'd come back up the stairs. There was a time when I couldn't climb the stairs on my own and Beth would have to help me. I would get outside, regardless of the weather, walk as far as I could, sit down and rest, walk some more and rest, and do the same on the return home. Over a period of about three months, I was able to improve my exercise tolerance to the point that I could walk twenty minutes without resting. The ability to move was exhilarating and encouraging, so I continued to increase my time and distance. I had always heard that exercise was a great mood elevator, but now I knew it firsthand. I took my last dose of prednisone in June of 2003.

It was a tough time for me. Despite Beth being so loving and supportive, I had become depressed and angry. I was struggling through the stages of grief. Finally, I accepted my loss and started coming out of it. Very few people regain their full capacity of strength and energy after experiencing generalized MG. Most people get depressed and can't seem to fight their way back. It was very tough but the Lord was with me and anything is possible if he's got your back.

I continued to fly my 5552XRAY even with MG. Because of the MG, I was required to take a medical exam every six months, and I did this for two years. After the two-year period, I was approved for a second-class medical certificate, and then I had to be tested only every two years. That is when I learned how many extremely ill physicians are flying with conditions such as previous heart attacks, strokes, and conditions much more problematic than MG.

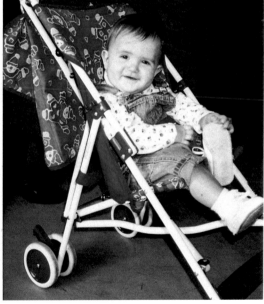

Top, Lauren and Bill, Matthew and Rhonda, Caroline and Tommy enjoying the pool, 1997. *Bottom left,* Katie, Matthew, Caroline, Lauren, and Papa on four-wheeler, 1998. *Bottom right,* Katie at her first cattle sale, 1997.

MEDICINE IS ONLY PART OF THE CURE

That my complete cure was divinely driven I am sure. But I believe self-discipline and a positive attitude played a huge part. Telling myself "I think I can" versus "I think I can't." The source of my positive attitude is probably partly my DNA, partly my religion, and partly a practice I have honed, beginning with my reading of Norman Vincent Peale's book *The Power of Positive Thinking* as a teenager. It's been essential in my entrepreneurial efforts because you can't sell unless you believe in what you're selling. I've been extremely successful, seldom failing in anything I have started: Henderson & Walton, the satellites, the Surgical Center, Southeast Health Plan, and MediSphere. Success also stems from hiring people with that same trait of positive thinking. If you hire people who have a positive "can-do" attitude, success will follow. If you hire a bunch of duds, they'll just tear you down. Always be on the lookout for people who are dedicated to moving forward and are smarter than you.

I also believe that what brought on the MG was that I had overloaded my boat. I had too much going on. Stress, worry, and pushing yourself beyond healthy limits can tear down your immune system. It's imperative to exercise, pray, mediate, rest, whatever you need to do to reduce stress. Beth had been telling me, "You're working too hard, you're not taking care of yourself, not exercising enough…" and it caught up with me. Many of my friends are having strokes, heart attacks, and dying. For most of them, it's self-induced; they're either smoking, overeating, or not exercising. Now, I walk daily and work out with a trainer three times a week. It is a mood elevator and is essential for healthy longevity.

FUTURE BEEF, 2000–2001

Overall, I am pleased with the wide swath I have cut in the entrepreneurial arena. However, one effort begun during my illness resulted in a bitter, painful experience. In 2000, I invested in the idea of vertically integrating the cattle business. The founders of a company called Future Beef had approached me as owner of Twin Valley Farms, LLC, to supply their operation with beef. The plan was to, under one roof, process all parts of the cow—from the high-quality meat, to the leather, to the hooves—and turn it all into products to sell. The founders had pulled together the most forward-thinking people in the beef business. Beth didn't want me to do it because I was still sick, but everything seemed to be falling together. Beth and I put in $1.5 million of our own funds, and I helped to raise

Top left, Ron, Beth, Lauren, and Caroline, 1996. *Top right,*
Beth holding granddaughter Caroline, 1996. *Bottom left,*
Ron holding Caroline, 1996. *Bottom right,* Ron riding
horse named Bo at Twin Valley Farms, 1996.

almost $35 million dollars from others. The fundraising effort led to my being elected as the CEO of Future Beef.

We built a $100 million, 450,000-square-foot, state-of-the-art facility in Arkansas City, Kansas. Just prior to our opening, the bottom had dropped out of the cattle market, and we were already losing money on each steer. But we had purchased the equipment and hired the staff, so went ahead and pulled the trigger on August 1 of 2001. Then the terrorist attacks of September 11th occurred, and everything shut down. Safeway, the nation's second-largest supermarket chain and our exclusive customer, backed out of its contract. Everybody stopped buying stuff, everybody stopped traveling—it was a disaster.

The September 11th terrorist attacks sent an already faltering cattle market into a downward spiral from which we couldn't recover. Three months later, Future Beef declared Chapter 11 bankruptcy and laid off nine hundred employees. By our first anniversary in August of 2002, the courts ordered the company into Chapter 7 bankruptcy liquidation. We lost everything. I didn't have the farm invested, thank God. But everything we had put in financially, all my efforts, salesmanship, and travel had not been enough.

When Safeway backed out of its contract, we had no money with which to litigate it. I learned several valuable lessons. In contrast to my previous successful endeavors, I was dealing with people with whom I had no close relationships or ties, particularly the founding members of Future Beef who were mostly academics. Another lesson I learned was if it's you against the world, bet on the world. Sometimes the cards are just stacked against you. A lot of people got hurt a lot worse than we did. But you can't piss and moan about it—you have to move on and certainly not dwell on fate. Just pick yourself up and keep moving forward. I still believe that had it not been for the tragedy of September 11th, we would have been a major success story rather than the failure that it proved to be. Building the company had been a therapeutic effort for me during my illness because I saw the value of vertical integration, and it gave me something to strive for. The plant in Arkansas City, Kansas, is still operating today under new owners.

Opposite top left, The Prattville Progress, 1997 (see full article on page 195). *Top right, The Birmingham News*, November 2001 (see full article on page 196). *Bottom left, Attacking Myasthenia Gravis, A Key in the Battle Against Autoimmune Disease*, by Ronald E. Henderson, 2003. *Bottom right,* Invitation to fundraiser for Myasthenia Gravis Foundation, held at Twin Valley Farms, 2001.

Henderson rides herd on Twin Valley

By Barbara Knight
The Prattville Progress

Dr. Ron Henderson, owner of Twin Valley Farms near Prattville spent his formative years on his family's Autauga County cotton, corn and cattle farm.

Today Henderson is one of the most successful Angus beef cattle breeders in the country. He has also been a leader in women's health care. He specializes in gynecology, obstetrics and infertility at Birmingham's Henderson, Walton Women's Center (now Medisphere Health Partners), one of the largest and most unique private practices of its kind in the country. The center has satellite offices in seven central Alabama towns.

Henderson also founded a Birmingham-based physicians practice management company that has a national focus.

"I'm the luckiest guy in the world," he said. "My work is my hobby. I love medicine. I love people. And I have a tremendous love for agriculture, particularly farming. I have been able to combine all these things."

Henderson's knowledge has served to develop a premiere operation in Autauga County that could serve as a "poster child" for modern farming. The farm's 3,000 owned and leased acres are home to 1,400 head of cattle.

In 1964 Henderson bought half-interest in his family's 116-acre home-place farm. He purchased the Ward Farm on

(Please see FARM, page 2)

Lisa Bundy/Staff

Dr. Ron Henderson looks over some of the herd at his Twin Valley Farms in Autauga County. It's one of the nation's foremost Angus cattle operations.

NEWS STAFF/FRANK COUCH

J. Edwin Blalock, a professor of physiology and biophysics at the University of Alabama School of Medicine in Birmingham, stands in the lab where he's working on a cure for myasthenia gravis. With him is Dr. Ron Henderson, who has MG and is raising money for research into autoimmune diseases.

Looking for a cure
Myasthenia gravis victim seeks research funds

ATTACKING
MYASTHENIA GRAVIS

A Key in the Battle Against Autoimmune Diseases

By Ronald E. Henderson, M.D.

THE ALABAMA CHAPTER
MYASTHENIA GRAVIS FOUNDATION

PRESENTS

"ROUND UP A CURE"

HONORING
JAMES A. PITTMAN, M.D.

HOSTED BY
DR RON AND BETH HENDERSON

TWIN VALLEY FARMS
PRATTVILLE, ALABAMA

The Birmingham News

LIFESTYLE

Sunday
September 29, 2002

E

NEWS STAFF/BEVERLY TAYLOR

Dr. Ron Henderson of Birmingham dedicates his new book to his wife, Beth, as "the ultimate caregiver." An obstetrician-gynecologist, he retired with the expectation that he would die from myasthenia gravis and went into self-imposed isolation. He wouldn't have been able to come out of that without her, he says.

Illness gives new purpose

For ailing doctor, retirement wasn't the end but a beginning

By BETSY PRICE
News staff writer

Standing out among the sheet music on the grand piano in the Liberty Park home of Dr. Ronald E. Henderson and his wife, Beth, is "Go Tell It on the Mountain."

And he intends to.

The 65-year-old Birmingham obstetrician-gynecologist, who retired in 1994 because myasthenia gravis was taking its toll, has found a new lease on life.

His illness has given him a new cause: To spread the message that diet, exercise and medication can help the chronically ill lead a better life. He's also helping to raise money that targets research to help not only his illness, but all autoimmune disorders in which the body attacks itself, such as thyroid problems, diabetes, multiple sclerosis, rheumatoid arthritis.

He has a few irons in the fire, typical of the man who used to practice medicine, help operate an insurance company and run Henderson-Walton Women's Center, an OB-GYN physician-management group, among other things.

Henderson has written a book about living with myasthenia gravis and chronic illness, "Attacking Myasthenia Gravis: A Key in the Battle Against Autoimmune Diseases" (Court Street Press, $25.95). He's

DETAILS

▶ **What:** Dr. Ronald E. Henderson, a Birmingham obstetrician-gynecologist and businessman, signing his new book, "Attacking Myasthenia Gravis: A Key in the Battle Against Autoimmune Disease." (Court Street Press, $25.95).

▶ **Where:** Henderson & Walton Women's Center, sixth floor of the Women and Children's Center in front of St. Vincent's Hospital, 806 St. Vincent's Drive.

▶ **When:** Monday, 8-10 a.m.; noon-2 p.m.; 4-6 p.m.

formed a foundation that will raise money for and fund research to combat autoimmune disorders. And he's launched a Web site to support it all — www.IADR.org.

"I've always wanted to make a difference," Henderson says.

His new book contains lessons not just for those with chronic illness, but everybody living in today's harried and overpressured world.

Henderson used to strive to make a difference in the health care system, which he considers so broken that neither physician nor patient can make it work without great effort.

▶ **See Henderson, Page 5E**

Daily dozen helps control life's challenges

Dr. Ronald E. Henderson's 12 rules for taking control of any chronic illness also apply to life in general and the "challenges — not problems" we all face, he believes. Here is a summary of his rules:

▶ **Educate yourself about your disease.** You must take control of your life, and knowing what is going on is a key factor. You hire doctors and others to help you — but they are not living with it every day. Learn the general course of the illness. Know what the medications are. Keep up with new medicine and treatments.

▶ **Practice the four basic tenets of a healthy lifestyle.** Do not smoke. Maintain a normal body weight. Eat a balanced diet. Practice a daily disciplined regimen

of physical exercise. You can't change your genetics, but you can reduce risk factors, Henderson notes.

▶ **Practice mental exercise.** Use your noggin to research your disease, find a new hobby, cause or interest — even classes at community schools or area colleges. It's more important than ever to stay sharp, he says.

▶ **Balance rest with activity.** Remain active, but accommodate your body's changed needs. Don't get too much rest, however. That's counterproductive, he says.

▶ **Interact productively with your doctor or doctors.** You are the one who ultimately is in charge of your life and condition. Do not be afraid to ask your doctor

any questions you have and express yourself when you have doubts about a recommendation or don't understand what the doctor is doing. Another key: Once you and the doctor have agreed on a course of treatment, follow the doctor's advice.

▶ **Maintain a positive attitude.** Millions of people with chronic illnesses lead productive lives. You can, too, Henderson says. "You can turn lemons into lemonade." Look at actor Christopher Reeve, who has reported having feeling in limbs that should not, he notes.

▶ **See Dozen, Page 5E**

ATTACKING MYASTHENIA GRAVIS

The Birmingham News, September 29, 2002. *(continued on page 197)*

BIRMINGHAM
BUSINESS JOURNAL

Doctor-turned-patient turns philanthropist

TOM BASSING

Nearly eight years ago, Ron Henderson convinced himself he had been handed a death sentence. His health was failing, and he took stock of his symptoms.

He was fatigued, sometimes to the point of incapacitation, and he grew certain he would die in the grim manner of New York Yankees great Lou Gehrig: All semblance of energy would vanish; his muscles would wither; he would be unable to swallow, then to breathe; and he would die.

Amyotrophic lateral sclerosis, or Lou Gehrig's disease as it came to be known after the Yankee Hall of Famer's death in 1941 at the age of 37, affects an estimated 30,000 Americans at any given time.

Henderson, then a 57 year-old Birmingham physician, figured he had, at best, five years to live.

It had to be ALS.

How else to explain what was happening to him, to a doctor who had preached and practiced preventive medicine, who had never smoked, who ate right, who began his day at 4 a.m. with a regimen of meditation and rigorous exercise. A man with the energy to be, at once, a physician, an entrepreneur and a family man. A man who, on average, needed a mere five or six hours of sleep a night.

A man who now lacked the pep to even get out of bed some days. Whose muscles had grown so fatigued, he couldn't keep his head erect.

"It feels like gravity is three G's. You don't want to get up," Henderson recounts. "I couldn't tie my shoes; I couldn't even button my own shirt."

It had to be ALS. Yet, it wasn't.

Seeking a cure

Henderson had missed his own diagnosis.

Months later, in November 1995, he received the correct diagnosis, myasthenia gravis (MG), a disease for which similarly there is no cure, but which, for a time, can be managed. No guarantee for how long.

Myasthenia gravis is an autoimmune disease in which a person's anti-invasion shock troops turn traitor and attack the very body they're intended to defend.

Autoimmune diseases include MG, lupus, multiple sclerosis, psoriasis, rheumatoid arthritis and type 1 diabetes, among others, all of which ▫ combined ▫ affect millions of Americans.

Virtually all of the myriad autoimmune diseases have their own foundations to fund research into potential cures.

However, Henderson, now 65, is in the vanguard of a growing cadre of clinicians and research scientists who suspect a cure for one autoimmune disease will prove a cure for many others, and his new foundation is designed to fund any promising research into any of the various autoimmune diseases.

"We're confident that if we find an excellent treatment or even cure for one, it will be applicable to all these diseases," he says. "I'm the eternal optimist, but this is not just my opinion: We're very close to finding a cure for autoimmune diseases in general.

"If you break the seal, so to speak, on one autoimmune disease, you break the seal for many others."

Forming a foundation

While some people might take such a devastating diagnosis lying down, Henderson is the sort who would rather fight.

"Our family came from stock that didn't have self-pity," he says. "Our parents instilled in us a sense of self-reliance."

So it is that Henderson the patient has founded the International Autoimmune Disease Research Foundation, which, he says, is unique in its funding strategy.

Most health-related foundations hold on to their principal and use accrued interest to award research and information grants.

Henderson's is a so-called pass-through foundation, by which all funds raised will be doled out to finance various research projects.

"The foundation is going to be a zebra among ponies," he says.

Who wins funding will be determined by the foundation's board of scientists, an international group of multidisciplinary researchers.

"There's a commonality to these disorders, a cross-section of diseases that fit under the rubric of immune disorders," says Dr. Charles Garrison Fathman, who is the director of the Center for Clinical Immunology at Stanford University and the founding chairman of the foundation's scientific board. "We'll vet the applications to decide which are the best candidates for research funding."

Pushed to succeed

Henderson was born in July 1937 on what he describes as "a dirt farm" in south-central Alabama, and it was there that he first learned his work ethic. Money was scarce; toil was not.

His parents pushed him and his brothers to attend college; Henderson took it a step further, earning his medical degree from the University of Alabama in 1962.

He founded an obstetrics and gynecology clinic in Birmingham, which later evolved into a 15-physician practice known as the Henderson & Walton Women's Center on the St. Vincent's Hospital campus.

He also founded a physician practice management firm, MediSphere Corp.

And then illness befell him. In November 1994, he reluctantly quit practicing medicine. Even today, he says, "I miss practicing medicine so much I can taste it."

He turned his focus to strengthening MediSphere even as fatigue began to overwhelm him. Eventually, he sold the company to a Tennessee firm.

Now, he spends his time at book signings ▫ proceeds from his recently completed memoir and examination of his illness, Attacking Myasthenia Gravis, go to the foundation ▫ and soliciting potential donors.

Medication and his focus on the foundation have invigorated him.

"I feel great. I do get frustrated because I was born with high energy and high curiosity, and now I have to pace myself," he says. "In a lot of ways, it's mind over matter. You have to appreciate what you have left."

A powerful team

The Internal Revenue Service this year accorded the foundation nonprofit status, and already Henderson has begun assembling an administrative board of trustees and a board of scientists, which will vet the research-funding applications.

The Birmingham-based foundation will hold its "first board meeting in the first quarter of 2003," says Henderson, who expects to raise $15 million the first year and $50 million by year five. Moreover, he says, "I'm committed to matching $250,000" from his own pocket.

"We've got a large number of people with autoimmune diseases, and that expresses the need for greater research," Stanford's Fathman says. "The federal government contributes a lot of money to this type of research, but private foundations are an important source of additional funding."

Fathman, who also chairs the Federation of Clinical Immunology Scientists, is the sort of scientific heavyweight Henderson has attracted to his undertaking.

Dr. Bill Roper is another. The current dean of the School of Public Health at the University of North Carolina at Chapel Hill has agreed to join the foundation's board of trustees. He formerly served on the senior White House staff during the Reagan administration and directed the Centers for Disease Control and Prevention during the senior Bush's presidential term.

He was persuaded to take on his new responsibilities because of his respect for, and longtime friendship with, Henderson.

"I've known Ron Henderson for 25 years," Roper says, "and he is extremely dedicated to any project he takes on. That's why he'll succeed."

The Birmingham Business Journal, December 15, 2002.

Earl and Sara at their new home on Green Crest Road, 1970.

CHAPTER 10

OUR PARENTS' TWILIGHT YEARS

A s our parents aged, we did the best we could to take care of them while we raised our own children and navigated my career. Beth and I, while I was practicing in Gordo, bought half interest in the homeplace farm, which allowed my parents to buy a new home. Mother had been insisting on remodeling the homeplace, while Daddy was resisting her efforts. Beth and I dropped by one Sunday afternoon and told them that if they could find a house they liked, we'd pay one and a half times that amount for the land, with the idea that the additional money could furnish the house.

That evening we had not even unloaded the car when the phone rang. Mother said that they had found a house that they wanted to buy. They bought a newly built house on the property once owned by Papa Henderson that he had sold to the real estate entrepreneur Mr. Mac Murphy. From this vantage point, Mother and Daddy could still see Papa's old block house, which was just across Highway 31 from the homeplace. Mother was a very proud woman, and she wanted her new home to look nice. She took a portion of the money and furnished the house beautifully.

Even in their latter years, my mother and father had a wonderful relationship. But the last ten years of my father's life were tough. After his boys moved out and he lost his free labor, the farm grew up around him. He retired from farming and started selling insurance on a debit basis, collecting door-to-door each month. When we purchased TVF, Daddy oversaw the cattle and managed the farm during the week for at least two years.

Eventually, Mother and Daddy both got sick with emphysema, as they were nicotine addicts. In his last years, when his emphysema was bad, Daddy would go to our old homeplace just to keep his mind active. In the woods, he dug up sapling water oaks, maples, persimmons, and plum trees and planted them on the homeplace site, pampering them. He knew how to plant a tree, what you did for prep, and all the materials you put around it. The saplings Daddy planted are now huge, beautiful trees.

During Daddy's long and painful final illness, Mother again became a loving and devoted caregiver. Her entire existence was consumed by his needs until his death at seventy-seven years of age. In the months before he died, I brought him to see my friend and pulmonologist, Dr. Terrell Spencer, who ran tests to see if there was anything else they could do about his lungs. But his lungs were just gone. He was really sick and needed to be on oxygen more than he was off.

In February of 1987, when I determined he was terminal, I worked out a rotation schedule with my brothers so someone was always with our parents at the house, where we had installed a hospital bed. My youngest brother, Tommy, came from his home in Shreveport, Louisiana, and stayed with them a week. My brother Jerry, who was living in San Francisco, came and stayed the next week. Then I sent Beth to stay during my week because I was working. I was also running for a spot on the board of the American Medical Association, and we were hosting the AMA president. And so I asked Beth to return to Birmingham on Wednesday night for a dinner, leaving only Mother with Daddy, with him so sick. Beth came back, and we had a delightful dinner. Early the next morning, my daddy died. Mother was by herself, which was heartbreaking for me. But he had a courageous death. I remember the last time I saw him, on Sunday when I was down during Beth's week, and he'd quit eating. I said, "Daddy, if you don't eat, you're going to die." No response. I said, "Daddy, how long do you want to live?" He leaned forward on his elbows so he could get more breath and said, "As *long* as I can," just as angry as he could be. But he was not afraid of death.

Top left, Ron, Jerry, and Tommy with Sara
and Earl at their 50th wedding anniversary
celebration in the conference room at Twin
Valley Farms, 1986. *Top right,* Ron visiting
Sara and Earl at their home on Green Crest
Road, Prattville, Alabama, 1986. *Bottom left,*
Earl and Sara and grandchildren Rhonda,
Bill, and Ellen, late 1986. *Bottom right,* Sara
visiting house on Old Leeds Road to attend
a wedding party for Rhonda, 1991.

Mother remained proud of her sons, all three graduates of the University of Alabama, throughout her life. Gerald retired after thirty years as senior vice president of Chevron International, based in California. Tom had a career as an electrical engineer at International Paper in Louisiana. And I was a doctor. Anyone who was around her for any length of time had to suffer through her bragging about her children. Her bragging rights extended to her grandchildren when they came along. She was always interested in how their education was progressing. On my frequent weekly visits and phone calls, she always wanted a report on each family member. In her last four years, the arrival of four great-grandchildren was absolutely joyous for her. She was failing in health by this time, and when the young children were around she would alternatively laugh and cry, saying, "I don't understand this, except I just am overwhelmed by my love for them."

Mother passed away on Mother's Day in 1997, at seventy-nine years of age, also from emphysema. Following our annual beach trip, Beth and I had driven back down to Florida to retrieve the plane that had been left there due to bad weather. I kept calling mother periodically, but I couldn't get her to answer the phone. So I flew back to Prattville and drove straight to her house. I found her at home, deceased. Just two weeks prior, at a family gathering, she had held her newest great-granddaughter, Katie.

Earlier in her life, she had had endometrial cancer because she took estrogen unopposed, and that is a prescription for that result. She needed a hysterectomy, and Ernie Moore did the surgery, but I assisted. I thought it would be a strange feeling removing the womb that I came here in, but it didn't faze me one bit. It didn't faze her either; she wanted me there. And except for that, she had never had cancer, stroke, or heart attack, even with the nicotine. I think that speaks highly of my genetic makeup.

I feel the presence of my parents often. I miss both of them, but Daddy and I were so close I probably miss him more often. Mother was more of a preacher than a teacher. She advocated for what she wanted done. Daddy would work the example and show me how to do it, so we built more of a relationship.

Beth's parents also lived long, full lives. Mr. Summerville worked in his barbershop until he was about sixty-eight years old. He had such a welcoming personality that folks would come into his shop just to visit. They'd sit and talk while he cut hair. Beth's immense compassion for others comes from him. In his late fifties, he had begun having chest pains; I diagnosed him with angina and prescribed nitroglycerine since heart catheters were

Top: Sara and her three sons, Tommy, Jerry, and Ron, in California at Jerry's daughter Tracy's wedding, 1994. *Bottom left,* Colley Summerville at home in Prattville, 1985. *Bottom right,* Colley and Elizabeth Summerville, his birthday, 1985.

not yet available. He died a couple of days after his eightieth birthday in 1986, after having his first angiogram. The dye used in the procedure interfered with his oxygen supply to his heart, and he had a fatal heart attack. He was a great supporter of mine, and I loved him dearly.

Beth's mother, Carrie Elizabeth Garthright Summerville, was a wonderful mother for Beth in a lot of ways. Mrs. Summerville was attractive, well dressed, and really promoted family values. In 2000, at eighty-nine, she was admitted to a Montgomery hospital following a massive coronary with uremia, or kidney failure. As she worsened, she had to be put on a ventilator. With no improvement after several days, we made the hard decision to take her off the ventilator. Beth wanted to place a no-resuscitate order on her charts, and I agreed. She was placed in a room and expected to die. However, she regained consciousness. So we took her to the farm and set up a hospital bed in my office downstairs. Uremia is actually a beautiful way to go because you become happy and jovial. But she was aphasic, which means she couldn't think of the words she needed, couldn't talk. During that last month, Beth and I took care of all of her needs ourselves. She was so petite and lovely, smiling at us all the while. As a physician, I felt it was my responsibility to handle the medical needs, and I wanted to do it. It was a beautiful death, and it bonded us.

My friend Joe Chambliss's mother, my "Aunt Gladys," passed away in 1999. She was a wonderful woman who offered me love, encouragement, and acceptance throughout my entire life. She was the glue that kept her family together through the hard times, always preaching family first. And she made sure that I knew I was a part of the clan. At her death, the family asked me to present the eulogy, which was an incredible responsibility and honor for me.

Top, Mrs. Summerville holding Matthew at his first cattle sale at Twin Valley Farms, 1994. *Center,* Elizabeth "MawMaw" Summerville, Rhonda, Ellen, and Sara, 1991. *Bottom,* Beth and her mother, Elizabeth, at a TVF cattle sale, 1994.

An excerpt from:
A Eulogy for Gladys Wadsworth Chambliss
December 22, 1999

By Ron Henderson

. . . Aunt Gladys. Aunt Gladys. I can't remember not knowing that sound and the connotations that that wonderful sound meant to me. You see, Aunt Gladys was not my aunt. She came into my life through her firstborn son, my friend "Little Joe." Beginning in the first grade and through my college years, I was an overnight guest in her home two to three times every month, as well as a regular visitor on special, and not so special, occasions. She always treated me just like a member of her core family, and I was made to feel very special by her warmth, generosity, and love. Her home was a marvelous place to be—a beehive of activity, where mutual respect was taught and practiced by her entire family. An atmosphere of love and kindness exuded from Aunty Gladys and permeated the entire home.

In 1948, Aunt Gladys and Uncle Joe bought a store, the Chambliss Texaco Grocery on Highway 14. A full-time occupation, Aunt Gladys ran the store and the family simultaneously, in an almost seamless fashion. Oftentimes, in their physically attached home and business, it was difficult to determine who was a customer and who was a guest. I was not the only one who experienced this confusion. A tremendous warmth and love surrounded the place—for people of all walks of life, be they poor or rich, black or white. There was a great deal of outright philanthropy practiced by the Chambliss family. In a very generous and often transparent manner, credit was granted with a mutual understanding that the financial debt would never be repaid. Such was the generosity of my saintly Aunt Gladys.

I continued to visit Aunt Gladys even while attending college. Being in her presence was very comforting and energizing to me, and I was made to believe that she was very happy to see me regardless of the timeliness of my visit. After she sold the store, our paths didn't cross as often. She knew, and her family knew, that I was there for her if my services were ever needed. During the past year, I have been able to be of some help to her, with advice and influence, but never could I repay her for the positive impact she made on my life.

. . . I will personally miss Aunt Gladys, but will forever be guided by what she taught me by being a living model of a life well lived.

Top, Ron's "Aunt Gladys" Chambliss, about 1960. *Bottom,* Memorial service program cover, 1999.

Top, Dr. Ed Partridge, vice chairman of the Department of Obstetrics and Gynecology at the University of Alabama in Birmingham, 2010. *Bottom,* Dr. John C. Hauth, chairman of the Department of Obstetrics and Gynecology at the University of Alabama in Birmingham, 2003.

CHAPTER 11

A LIFELINE FROM TWO GREAT PHYSICIANS AND DEAR FRIENDS

2004–2009

In February of 2004, I had been off all immunosuppressants for eight months. I called Drs. John C. Hauth and Ed Partridge, chairman and vice chairman of the Department of Obstetrics and Gynecology at the University of Alabama in Birmingham, and asked if I could volunteer my time to the department. The next day, I was sitting in Dr. Hauth's office with both of them, explaining my situation and my intense desire to get back to work. They said there would be an opening for me in the summer. The person who had been running the outpatient clinic was leaving in June, and I was asked to replace her. I asked Dr. Hauth what I would be doing and he responded, "Well, you'll do everything!"

In August, I began a full-time job as a professor of obstetrics and gynecology, with a significant salary included. I'd been out of the operating room for ten years, and Dr. Partridge was to proctor me back into the OR. The second day of observing my surgical skills, he said, "Hell, Ron, you're ready to go back now." And I did. I was responsible for overseeing all of the outpatient clinics, but primarily the Russell Clinic at UAB. All third- and fourth-year residents rotated through the clinic, and I scrubbed in to surgery with them. On Tuesday mornings and Thursday afternoons, no patient appointments were scheduled so that we could schedule surgery.

My expertise was vaginal surgery. I have done, by a stopwatch, a simple vaginal hysterectomy (the uterus only, close the cuff) in nine minutes. Phil Walton was on one side and a second-year resident on the other. Phil took a video of it, which I still have. I have very good eye-hand coordination. Doctors with good eye-hand coordination can operate quickly. Three fine doctors helped me hone my surgical skills. When I was in Gordo, Dr. Floyd Fitts of Tuscaloosa would come to my hospital, North Pickens Hospital in Reform, and handle my major surgery cases with me assisting. No one had ever done major surgery in North Pickens Hospital, so we had to upgrade the aesthesia and equipment. Floyd taught me, "Plan your move and don't have any wasted movement." Dr. Paul "Papa Doc" Salter had the same incredible eye-hand coordination as Floyd Fitts. I had gotten to know Paul Salter when he was attending on the twelfth floor of the University Hospital. These guys were just good. Dr. Robert "Bob" May was my attending in my second year of residency. If I made a wrong move, he'd hit me on the hand with an instrument and say, "You don't need to do that." He was out-standing. I became a good assistant watching him assist, and in turn, he always asked me to assist. Those three people really helped to develop my surgical skills. Basically though, it's a God-given talent, you either have it or you don't. Some of the best academic people are in academia because they can't compete in private practice—they just don't know how to get in and get the job done.

You also have to have good eye-hand coordination to master laparoscopy, an operation performed in the abdomen or pelvis through a small incision using a camera. My colleague Dr. Frank Page is one of the best laparosco-pists I have ever known. I did the first laparoscopy procedure in the state of Alabama in 1968. Dr. Erskin Carmichael was on the full-time St. Vincent's staff and had gone to Columbia University Medical Center for a month-long externship to learn laparoscopy. He was going to teach all of us how to perform the procedure. We scheduled a patient and he asked me, chief resident at the time, to assist. And he couldn't get the damn needle in the belly. So I ended up doing it. I have that God-given dexterity. I can pick blueberries at the farm using each hand just as easily as the other. I can feel the berry to see if it's ready by size and consistency. You develop that sensitivity when you can't keep eyes on both hands. Either my ancestors had the same traits or we developed it picking cotton. My daddy had good hands, and my brother Jerry could always pick more cotton than I could.

For the next five years, I thoroughly enjoyed my experience at UAB. When I surpassed the mandatory age of retirement, seventy, and I was seventy-two, I was gently asked to retire. Dr. Kirklin had implemented the retirement policy. Dr. Hauth told me, "Ron, I have protected you for two

Henderson Receives MASA Award

The recipient of the **Howard L. Holley Award** was **Ronald E. Henderson, MD**, of Birmingham.

Ronald Henderson, MD

The award recognizes Alabama physicians who have made significant contributions to the understanding and appreciation of medicine through non-technical published or broadcast works.

Dr. Henderson has been a medical leader and an entrepreneur for three and a half decades. He was the founder and longtime chief executive officer of Henderson & Walton Women's Center in Birmingham, one of the largest freestanding obstetrics and gynecology practices in the Southeast.

In 1994, Dr. Henderson was forced to retire because of symptoms of the rare muscle-weakness disease known as myasthenia gravis. Since his diagnosis, Dr. Henderson established the International Autoimmune Disease Research Foundation, which is dedicated to research in the field of autoimmune diseases, including myasthenia gravis. He also wrote a book – *Attacking Myasthenia Gravis: A Key in the Battle Against Autoimmune Diseases*. All profits from the sale of the book go to the foundation and its battle against autoimmune diseases. The book has assisted researchers and physicians as they work to find a cure for autoimmune diseases.

Dr. Henderson has been active in physician organizations serving as a member of the Board of Censors of the Medical Association of the State of Alabama and as president of MASA from 1982-1983. He also served on MASA's Alabama Delegation to the American Medical Association and was an elected member of the AMA's Council on Medical Service. He has been an active member of the Jefferson County Medical Society, and the American College of Obstetricians and Gynecologists. He was appointed by Congress to serve on the Physicians Payment and Medical Technology Board and later served on the State Health Planning and Development Agency Board. He co-founded the Birmingham Surgical Center and later founded the health maintenance organization Southeast Health Plan, as well as the physician practice management company, Medisphere Health Partners Inc.

Alabama MD, The Medical Association of State of Alabama, 2003.

years and can no longer do so." I reluctantly retired from an emotionally rewarding practice experience. Dr. Hauth seemed saddened to see me go.

The practice of medicine has afforded me an exciting and rewarding career. God put me here to be a doctor, and I think I did a good job. It was satisfying for me—like when I chopped cotton. I liked the results, how many rows I chopped. I had an endpoint. In practice, I could count the deliveries I had made and the surgeries I had performed. Taking into consideration my med school years, my residency, my time in Gordo, and my practice, I've delivered somewhere north of ten thousand babies. In my practice, the most deliveries I ever made in a single month was fifty-six, wall-to-wall, one after another. And I got to share in each family's joy at the birth of their baby.

I think my kids, as they were growing up, were proud of what I did. I was concerned that none of them would go into medicine because of my work ethic, being gone a lot at night and missing family events. Particularly Rhonda, who got really upset with me one day because I had to leave her special event to deliver a baby. And yet, Rhonda is the one who became a physician. But the practice of medicine is more flexible these days; many offices use the team approach and flextime. Even in my last five years at Henderson & Walton, we were becoming more adaptable. Several of our grandchildren are studying to be in medical fields—and I wouldn't change a thing. I think medicine is the most hallowed profession that one could aspire to enter. I feel very blessed that they're interested in health care.

Recognizing Excellence
1998-2010

HEALTHCARE
ALABAMA
HALL OF FAME

2010 Awards Luncheon
MAY 8, 2010
ALABAMA ACTIVITY CENTER
MONTGOMERY, ALABAMA

2010 Awards Luncheon

Induction Ceremony, Class of 2010

Invocation
rk Springer, Chaplain, Jackson Hospital and Clinic, Inc.

Luncheon

Welcome and Introduction of Special Guests
Wayne H. Finley, Ph.D., M.D.

Special Remarks
Ms. Bari Watson, B.A., M.A.

Introduction of Committee Members
Donald Ball, President

Presentation of Inductees by Committee Members

ıp, M.D...Neal E. Christopher, M.D.
Carl A. Grote, Jr., M.D...................................Wayne H. Finley, Ph.D.,M.D.
Madeline G. Harris, R.N., M.S.N.............................Rachel Z. Booth, Ph.D.
Ronald E. Henderson, M.D..........................Wayne H. Finley, Ph.D., M.D.
Florence A, Hixson, Ed.D.†..Ruth Harrell, R.N.
Thomas W. Jones, D.D.S.†...Joseph O. Dean, Ph.D.
William Holcomb (Hoke) Kerns, Sr.............E. Chandler Bramlett, F.A.C.H.E.
Margaret Israel Millsap, Ed.D., R.N.†........................Rachel Z. Booth, Ph.D.
Alice McNeal, M.D.†...Byron Green, M.D.
William Self Propst...Joseph O. Dean, Ph.D.
Leon Victor McVay, Jr.†..Louie C. Wilson, M.D.
Betty W. Vaughan, M.D..Neal E. Christopher, M.D.
John R. Wheat, M.D., M.P.H........................Wayne H. Finley, Ph.D., M.D.
John Allan Wyeth, M.D.†...Byron Green, M.D.

† deceased

Alabama Health Care Hall of Fame Luncheon program, 2010.

Beth, Ron, and Rocky, 2013.

CHAPTER 12

REINVENTING MYSELF IN RETIREMENT

2009

My Beth continued to be concerned about my flying, and in 2006, with a lot of sadness, I sold the airplane. By then, I no longer had my business ventures to which to expense trips, and the price of fuel had skyrocketed by more than fifty percent. It had become extremely expensive to fly, and I had to face the fact that the plane must be sold. I quickly canceled the leases on the hangers at 1A9 and BHM. I miss flying like a hungry man misses food to this very day. But, as I already said, you can't piss and moan about what life brings you, just deal with it.

So in 2009, at age 72, I needed to reinvent myself, and returned to my old private practice location, St. Vincent's Hospital Birmingham. The medical director offered me a lucrative position to be involved in a program in which we mildly and legally encouraged the physicians to use the hospital facilities more efficiently. After about six months, I became disenchanted with the program because I did not feel that it had any real value. At that time, I began my work on the Clinical Decision Unit, reviewing patient records for appropriate lengths of stay. Any patients that are admitted and do not qualify as inpatients based on strict criteria are called "observation patients." These observation patients take up beds and cause unnecessary expense when their workup can be done more efficiently as outpatients. I am still actively involved in this program and consider it meaningful work.

Since 2007, I have also been the medical director for Cahaba Safeguard Administrators, a company that tries to protect those in the health-care sector from fraud and abuse. In that role, I deal with many of the issues we battled through Southeast Health Plan, such as overbilling and over-charging for services rendered. In 2014, I dealt with the assistant attorney general for the state of Kentucky concerning a case where an optometrist was visiting nursing homes in his area to conduct monthly eye exams. He is not an ophthalmologist and has no ophthalmology contacts. I spent three days researching the laws of Kentucky to learn how an optometrist should be paid for just an exam, when they delivered no therapy. I recommended not only that they revoke the doctor's license but also arrest him for fraud. On the last call I got from the assistant attorney general, he said that the optometrist is still licensed but has stopped his abusive practices.

On my return to St. Vincent's, Bill Leitner, a urologist by training, had been established as the medical director. We have become very good friends. Bill has an absolutely outstanding professional brain and is hard-working with a strong moral center. He has a beautiful family, and he practices faith, family, and friends in that order. Bill is also very likeable, just plain fun to be around. He's always telling jokes and is a connoisseur of restaurants, which is a good quality to have in a friend! He and his wife, Dena, are our dear friends, and we enjoy spending time with them, particularly when we go out to dinner.

During this time, I have also become even closer to Terrell Spencer, who had long been my pulmonologist. His wife, Betty, was our real estate agent and my patient when I was practicing. Sadly, she passed away. And then Terrell's best friend died, and that's when I started having lunch with him every Thursday. In a small way, I was able to help him through that tough time. We still meet for lunch each Thursday and talk in between as well. We have a lot in common. He's a devout Christian, teaches Sunday school, and is hysterically funny. I call him "the mad scientist." He combs his hair but doesn't put gel on it, so when he goes out in the wind it blows all over the place and stands on end. He's now married to a lovely lady, Mary Roebuck Spencer, who sells real estate. Beth and I have taken several fantastic trips with them to Europe. Terrell's just a great guy and a lot of fun. I love him, and I've told him that.

I've also gotten to spend more time with my lifelong best friend, Joe Chambliss, visiting him and his wife at their home in Plantation, Florida. Joe married a beautiful woman named Gerri Maria, the daughter of an Italian family from Bessemer, Alabama. Joe first saw Gerri at an Alabama football game. He got one friend's notepad and another friend's camera and went up to her and said, "I'm from the *Birmingham News,* and I'd like to interview you and take your picture." That's how he was able to meet her. And she has been a supportive wife, a fantastic mother, and is devoted to her grandchildren.

Joe has had an incredibly successful career with Texaco Oil, ultimately developing service plazas on the Florida Turnpike. When he started with Texaco, his job was to entertain the executives. He would meet them at the airport and carry their baggage, getting to know all the upper brass. The chairman emeritus, A.C. Long, took a liking to Joe—he's easy to like. And for the first time in the history of the company, they allowed an employee to become an entrepreneur and take over several Texaco stations. When he first started, he'd arrive unexpectedly at the stations, put on a pair of white gloves, and run that white glove on the shelves and window-sills. If he found any dust, he'd raise hell with the managers to keep these places clean! Just a good businessman. The thing that is impressive about Joe is his ability to make friends with colleagues and employees, keep those friends, and still run the business properly.

At seventy-eight years old, he's still wide open—he is in excellent health and exercises daily. His company, the Chambliss Group, oversees stations on the Florida turnpike that now fly the Shell flag. He is, in every sense, a brother to me. To paraphrase our third president, Thomas Jefferson, "As I get older I find that I love the most the ones who I loved first." And that is really true.

Top left, Dr. William B. "Bill" Leitner. *Bottom left,* Dr. Terrell Spencer and Ron on trip to Scotland, 2013. *Bottom right,* Ron and Joe on the deck of the Chambliss' lake house, Lake Martin, Alabama, 2003.

Top, Henderson Family, Christmas, 2014. *Bottom*, Rhonda and
Tommy Powell and their children, Matthew and Caroline, 2014.

CHAPTER 13

OUR BEAUTIFUL FAMILY

Beth and I both had excellent parents who taught us family, moral, and Christian values—values we have passed on to our three children. Our children have grown up to be compassionate, independent, and responsible adults. They worked hard and made the most of their educational experiences. All three have established themselves professionally and done well. I also believe, because of our parenting and modeling, all three of them married well—they married Christians, soul mates who share their core values and common goals.

Rhonda graduated from Vanderbilt University with plans to go on to medical school. She didn't immediately get in, so she took some courses at UAB and got into medical school that next year. She practiced for three years in Jackson, Mississippi, while her husband, Tom Powell, an orthopedist and fantastic doctor, was in residency. We love Tommy like our own son. Tom now has a thriving practice at Brookwood Hospital. They moved back to Birmingham in 1996, when I was trying to manage the myasthenia gravis. Rhonda and I had planned to practice together. But she had one child and was pregnant with another and decided she wanted to be a full-time mom. When I told her I wasn't going to be able to practice with her, she said, "Whew! Daddy, I'm so relieved. I didn't know how I was going to tell you I wasn't going to practice with you."

Rhonda and Tommy gave us our first grandchild, Matthew Thomas, or "Papa's Boy." Before he was born, I wrote a prayer, "A Grandfather to Be," expressing my joy. Matthew is now a junior at Furman University and plans to go to med school. He is movie-star handsome and has great people skills. Rhonda and Tommy also have a beautiful daughter, Caroline Elizabeth, who is also extremely competent, bright, and confident. She has just started at Auburn University and is considering medical school. Whatever Caroline does, she will no doubt make the family proud.

Our younger daughter, Ellen, probably has the highest IQ of any of our children. She went to Vanderbilt University for a year but didn't like being in the shadow of her older sister. She transferred to Auburn University, marched in the Auburn University band, joined a sorority, and met a mentor who encouraged her to get an MBA at Syracuse University. She earned her MBA in finance, came back to Birmingham, and worked three years for BellSouth Corporation. One day she came to see me and said, "Dad, they've got 'golden handcuffs' on me. I've got a high salary, but I'm not happy." I said, "What you want to do?" And she said, "Go to law school." After three years at Vanderbilt School of Law and obtaining a JD degree, she came back to Birmingham and worked for seventeen years as a corporate defense litigator.

In 2005, Ellen married Jim Dover, who ran a successful insurance business and is a talented investor as well. Jim developed lymphoma in his late thirties, the treatment of which continues to have some health ramifications today. I love Jim like my own son, he's just a good guy. Jim and Ellen brought us our beautiful twins, James Ronald and Margaret Ann. Lively and intelligent, they will soon celebrate their ninth birthday. Ellen recently earned a master's degree in education and is teaching the fourth grade in Trussville. And the twins, in the first grade, are attending the same school with her.

Our son, Bill, received a business degree from the University of Alabama. He married Lyn Waggoner, who was my nurse at the HWWC practice. Lyn is extremely engaging, attractive, and intelligent—a spitfire standing 5'2". I love her dearly, just like my other two daughters. Lyn is now the events director for The Barn at Twin Valley Farms, responsible for leasing and overseeing the entire operation.

Bill joined the MediSphere team in 1994 as vice president of development and was integral to our recruitment of doctors into the program. He stayed on with MediSphere, even after the merger, until 1999. At the height of the TVF Angus cattle business, in 2000, we needed him at Twin Valley Farms to serve as CFO. Over the next three years, Bill totally upgraded the financial processes of our multimillion-dollar cattle business. He created a structured $2 million annual budget, including travel expenses in our tax reporting for the first time. In 2004, Bill ventured into the mortgage business, and a few years into it, the housing market crashed, undermining that part of the

Left, Jim and Ellen Dover and their children, Margaret Ann and James Ronald, 2014. *Right,* Lyn and Bill Henderson and their children, Lauren and Katie, 2014.

economy. He managed to make it in the business through even the worst years of the recession. In 2010, Bill went to work for Bank of America; when they pulled out of Alabama and Mississippi, he decided not to move with them to another state. He found a temporary position at St. Vincent's Birmingham and was soon promoted to director of supply.

Bill is as evenhanded and stable in business as he is as a son and father. Bill and Lyn's oldest daughter, Lauren Elise, is attending Mississippi College in nursing, with plans to become a nurse practitioner, which is very futuristic, since the supply of physicians is decreasing rapidly. Lauren has a real calling to be a missionary, so she'll probably get both degrees and work full-time in the mission field, serving as a nurse to the people of her country. Her younger sister, Katherine "Katie" Elizabeth, a gifted photographer and our free spirit, will be attending Mississippi College in the fall, pursuing a nursing degree and further education as a nurse anesthetist.

All four of my teenage grandchildren, my "covey" as I call them, are attractive, confident, and grounded. They are intellectually curious and keep themselves in good physical shape. I am sure the twins will follow suit. As I look to the future, my wish for my children and grandchildren is for them to continue to be the well-adjusted, balanced, financially secure individuals they are today and to always follow their passion.

In some regards, I think it is easier for self-made people to keep themselves grounded. My friend Joe Chambliss, from a similar background as me, started with next to nothing and built his business into a wildly successful enterprise. But Joe has kept his core values—he didn't get crazy—even though he's done an outstanding job. But if a person already has an elevated platform from which to work, whether it's financial or political, it's not like starting at the ground level and coming up. I think if you're given *too much* up front, without an understanding and appreciation of the big picture, you're more likely to run off the rails. If you look at financially successful families, the second generation may try to keep it in line, but the third generation heirs usually aren't good stewards of the wealth. They waste it away. I think there is an inherent responsibility to take it to the next level, to strive for a higher cause. It's not where you end up—it's how far you've come.

We spend a lot of time with the grandchildren talking about core values and setting goals. Every year, we spend a week together at the beach, all fourteen of us in the same house. It's just magical. Beth sets up an etiquette class, teaching the grandkids things like how to set the table and comportment. I post a big blue-and-white sign on an easel in the living room area to

Top, The first four, the "covey," Lauren, Katie, Caroline, and Matthew, with Ron and Beth, 2007. *Bottom left,* Henderson grandchildren, 2007: front row, from left, James and Maggie. Middle row: Caroline and Katie. Back row, Matthew and Lauren. *Bottom right,* Papa's School, held at the beach, 2005.

announce "Papa's School." I address all kinds of issues ranging from attitude to finance to current events. Our grown children even want to join in! I quiz them on subjects such as geography and the economy. I assign each grandchild a subject to research and report on, which is educational for the individual and the group. I also bring books for them to read, such as *The Power of Positive Thinking* by Norman Vincent Peale. Another past book was *Seven Habits of Highly Effective People* by Stephen Covey, which spells out the importance of setting goals and sub-goals. I wanted to impress upon them that a person is never through growing. Once I reach a goal, I immediately set a new one, and I would like for them to develop the same habit.

Ultimately, I don't want the grandchildren and future generations to feel that because they come from a financially strong family they don't have to give it their all in life. I want them to be motivated to succeed in their own rights. Anything can happen to an inheritance or to a spouse or to an economy. It is not only important for their financial stability, but for their own *self-esteem*. They should never take for granted what they have been given, but stay humble and grounded.

We also want them to understand the importance of philanthropy, of giving back. Beth and I have a goal to repay all of the organizations that helped us along the way. In 2000, Beth and I contributed the seed money to get the ball rolling on the construction of the Centennial Lodge at St. Vincent's, to provide comfortable housing for out-of-town patients and their families. I spearheaded the fundraising campaign to raise the $3.2 million needed for completion. Recently, Beth and I have made another donation to renovate the Lodge, which has seen a lot of traffic over the years. Civic responsibilities and contributions are essential if you want to live in a thriving, healthy environment.

The grandchildren are aware that their parents and grandparents have high expectations of them. But parenting and grandparenting is a work in progress; you're never finished. As I look at our grandchildren, I see young adults at the beginning of successful, fulfilling lives. I am so proud of them—I can't wait to see where they end up.

Opposite top left, St. Vincent's Foundation Digest, 1998 (see page 198 for larger article). Top right, The Prattville Progress, September 2006 (see page 199 for larger article). Bottom left, Front, from left, James, Beth, Rocky, and Maggie. Back, Lauren, Matthew, Ron, Caroline, and Katie, 2013. *Bottom right,* The Henderson family at the newly dedicated Guest Suite at University of Alabama's Bryant Hall Academic Center, 2006. Front row, from left: Ellen, Caroline, Katie, Lauren, Lyn, and Bill. Back: Jim, Beth, Ron, Matthew, and Tommy.

From left are: Beth Ann Henderson, Dr. Ronald Henderson and Mal Moore, the athletics director at the University of Alabama.

Former Autauga County Lion makes donation to U of A

By Jimmy White
Progress writer

Dr. Ronald E. Henderson, a native of Prattville, gave back to the University of Alabama in ceremonies held at the Bryant Hall on the grounds of the campus. In ceremonies held Sept. 8, Henderson presented the University with $250,000 for a Guest Suite at the University's Bryant Hall Academic Center. The gift matched his Prattville classmate, Joe Chambliss' gift of the same amount, for a guest suite.

The two guest suites are approximately 1,900 square feet and are used primarily by the University for overnight stays for dignitaries and special guests. A 1955 graduate of Autauga County High School, Henderson has been a medical leader and entrepreneur for three and half decades in Birmingham,

after graduating from the University's Medial College in 1962.

He is currently teaching at the University's School of Medical School in Birmingham. He is also active in a number of state and national organizations. Henderson was an OB-GYN specialist and founded the Henderson and Walton Women's Center in Birmingham, as well as a health maintenance organization.

After attending a November 2005 ceremony at Bryant Hall where his classmate at Autauga County High School, Joe Chambliss, gave $250,000 to the University's Crimson Foundation and a suite at Bryant Hall was named for the Chambliss Family, Henderson said he wanted to do something for the school.

"I had heard Dr. (Robert) Witt, the President of the University speak at the Birmingham Downtown Rotary Club about

the University going after the best and brightest and increasing the GPA of all students, including our student -athletes. My wife, Beth, and I had been looking for a way to give back to the University for all it had given us through the years. After hearing Dr. Witt and his vision for our campus, we wanted to help in any way we could. Then, seeing how my friend Joe Chambliss was able to help the athletic department convinced me to do he same thing."

Ronald Henderson grew up in Prattville, and played tight end for the Autauga County Lions. He played under the legendary Fred Jensen, lettering three seasons in three sports. He married his childhood sweetheart Beth Ann Summerville. They have two daughters, Dr. Rhonda H. Powell and Ellen H. Dover, and one son, William E. Henderson, and four grandchildren.

FALL 1998

FOUNDATION Digest

JOIN THE PARTY OF THE CENTURY!

It's a party 100 years in the making.

St. Vincent's Centennial Gala takes place November 7, 100 years to the month after the first four Daughters of Charity came to Birmingham and treated their first patients in a Southside mansion they had converted into a hospital.

One of the centerpieces of the Centennial Celebration, the Gala, will mark this momentous anniversary and extend St. Vincent's mission to the community by benefiting a new lodging facility for families of patients with special needs (see story on page 6).

The black tie affair will be held in a deluxe event tent on the lawn in front of the new Bruno Conference Center on the hospital campus.

Co-chairs of the Gala are **Dr. and Mrs. Merrill Bradley** and **Mr. and Mrs. Stanley Mackin**.

Dinner will be by **Chef Chris Hastings** of Hot and Hot Fish Club. Hastings was recently named one of the Best Regional Chefs by the Mondavi Winery. After-dinner dancing will be to the music of Al Belletto's New Orleans Jazz Band, featuring vocalist **Leif Pedersen**.

Tickets to the Gala are $250 per person with sponsored tables beginning at $2,000.

Photographed at the Gala preview party on July 30 are, from top left, 1) Mr. and Mrs. Stanley Mackin with Dr. and Mrs. Rex Harris, 2) Chef Chris Hastings of Hot and Hot Fish Club, 3) Dr. Ronald Henderson, Nina Botsford and Wayne Gillis and 4) Leif Pedersen and jazz band members.

CENTENNIAL
1898–1998

St.Vincent's
Foundation

The Vigil Newsletter

Spring 2015

Sisters' Vigil

Centennial Lodge, revisited:
Dr. Ron and Beth Henderson extend their torch-bearing legacy

Dr. Ron and Beth Henderson

When Ron Henderson, M.D., traces the history of St. Vincent's Centennial Lodge, he starts in the early 1990's, years before the 25-room facility became a mainstay for patients and families.

By that decade, this physician had become well aware of his patients' needs for hotel-style housing on the St. Vincent's Birmingham campus. Since Henderson & Walton Women's Center had grown to include seven geographically distant clinical offices, his patients scheduled for early-morning surgery at St. Vincent's often had to find pre-surgical lodging downtown.

Henderson, who was serving as chairman of what was then known as St. Vincent's Hospital Executive Committee, began advocating for on-campus lodging for patients and families. Others agreed, and his idea was included in the hospital's master plan. However, more pressing medical needs inevitably consumed available capital for a major project.

Thus, Henderson and his wife Beth decided they would spearhead a public effort with the support of the St. Vincent's Foundation. They not only contributed $100,000 toward the facility, but helped raise another $3.1 million.

As a result, Centennial Lodge opened December 14, 2000. It was immediately embraced by patients and their families across all service lines, especially families with a newborn in the Neonatal Intensive Care Unit. But the constant use took its toll. By the time the Hendersons' daughter accessed the Lodge to be near her hospitalized premature twins nearly ten years later, the family saw the wear and tear of thousands of overnight stays.

Henderson, who delivered more than 10,000 babies during his 30-year career, pondered what he and Beth might do to ensure the continued availability of convenient and affordable short-term housing.

"As a physician, I believe in what I call the 'Four C's' of health care: compassionate, competent, cost-effective, and convenient. The Lodge addresses convenience. It has been a blessing for a lot of people. Now I want to make sure the Lodge improves the experience for patients and families. That has been a consistent part of the Mission since I came to St. Vincent's in 1968, and I would like to see it sustained."

The Hendersons have therefore committed $500,000 to update Centennial Lodge. In appreciation of their repeated generosity, the renovated facility will be renamed The Ron and Beth Henderson Lodge.

cont. page 2

WHERE BABIES COME FROM:
EWCF supports maternity care

Every new life is a celebration. Every birth is a sacred event.

That's why St. Vincent's is so grateful to the Eastern Women's Committee of Fifty (EWCF), as its members help enhance those sacred celebrations at St. Vincent's East. The EWCF is donating its April 30 Highland Park Golf Tournament proceeds to St. Vincent's $6 million commitment to 18 state-of-the-art birth suites, a triage room, nursing education room, new waiting area, and improved Neonatal Intensive Care Unit space and equipment.

EWCF, a faithful community partner, has also supported the St. Vincent's East Cancer Center and other endeavors at St. Vincent's East. To learn how you or your organization can contribute toward the enhanced maternity experience at East—from wellness to lactation education—call 838-6151.

The Vigil Newsletter, St. Vincent's Foundation, Spring 2015. (continued on page 200)

APPENDICES

APPENDIX A

RONALD E. HENDERSON, MD
CURRICULUM VITAE

RESIDENCE

68 Cross Creek Drive East
Birmingham, Alabama 35213
(205)871-2770

FAMILY

Spouse: Beth Summerville Henderson

Children

Rhonda H. Powell, MD
Ellen H. Dover
William E. Henderson

Six Grandchildren

DATE/PLACE OF BIRTH

July 28, 1937
Prattville, Alabama

EDUCATION

University of Alabama, Tuscaloosa, Alabama
BS 1959

University of Alabama Medical College of Alabama, Birmingham, Alabama
MD 1962

Internship, Mixed Medicine, 1962–1963
University of Alabama Medical Center
University Hospital and Hillman Clinic
Birmingham, Alabama

Residency in Obstetrics and Gynecology (OB/GYN), 1965–1968
Chief Resident, 1967–1968
University of Alabama in Birmingham
The Medical Center/University of Alabama Hospitals and Clinics
Birmingham, Alabama

MEDICAL LICENSURE
1963, Alabama

SPECIALTY CERTIFICATION
American Board of Obstetrics and Gynecology
Certified: November 6, 1970

MEDICAL PRACTICE EXPERIENCE
Obstetrics and Gynecology, Henderson & Walton Women's Center, 1968–1994

St. Vincent's Hospital, Birmingham, Alabama, 1963–1965
Family Practice/Solo, Gordo, Alabama

FACULTY APPOINTMENTS
Medical College of Alabama (later University of Alabama in
Birmingham and then University of Alabama at Birmingham),
Department of Obstetrics and Gynecology

Clinical Professor, 2008 to present
Professor, active staff, July 2004–2008
Clinical Professor
Clinical Associate Professor
Clinical Assistant Professor
Clinical Instructor
Instructor

PROFESSIONAL EXPERIENCE IN ADDITION
TO MEDICAL PRACTICE/TEACHING

MediSphere Health Partners, Inc.   **Nashville, TN**   **1997–2001**
Chairman and Member of Board of Directors
- Chairman, February 1997–February 1998 (resigned due to health reasons)
- Member of Board of Directors, February 1997–January 2001
- Focus of company now on building and purchasing combination
  Surgicenters and Birthing Centers

MediSphere Corporation   **Birmingham, AL 1992–1997**
Founder, President, and CEO
- Practice management company that represented 50-plus physicians
  in Alabama, Georgia, Mississippi, and North Carolina
- MediSphere merged with Nashville startup company in February 1997,
  currently MediSphere Health Partners, Inc.

Southeast Health Plan   **Birmingham, AL 1984–1991**

Founder, Chairman, and CEO

- Chairman, 1984–1991
- CEO, 1984–1989
- First physician-owned Independent Practice Association/ Health Maintenance Organization (IPA/HMO) in the Southeast
- Southeast Health Plan introduced managed care to physicians in the state of Alabama

Birmingham Surgical Center   **Birmingham, AL 1983–1994**

Co-founder and Member of Board of Directors

- The first free-standing outpatient surgical care facility in the Southeast
- Major financial success. Instrumental in driving down cost of outpatient surgical procedures and stimulating hospitals to open same-day surgical units.

Mutual Assurance Society of Alabama   **Birmingham, AL 1976–1986**
(ProAssurance on the New York Stock Exchange)

Co-founder

- Physician-owned and -operated liability insurance company
- Member of Board of Directors; Member of Finance, Claims, and Underwriting Committees, 1976–1986

Henderson & Walton Woman's Center   **Birmingham, AL 1968–1994**

Founder and CEO

- Established what became the largest OB/GYN practice in Southeast
- Successfully grew the practice from three physicians and $2.7 million collected revenue in 1987 to 15 physicians and $12 million collected revenue in 1992. At end of my tenure, practice employed 19 physicians.
- Implemented a satellite office strategy with seven locations in Central Alabama, serving patients in a broad area of Central Alabama extending from West Georgia to East Mississippi
- Led practice in achieving "Accreditation with Commendation" designation from Joint Commission on Accreditation of Healthcare Organizations; Henderson & Walton Women's Center became first OB/GYN practice in the United States to achieve accreditation
- Retired from clinical practice in 1994 for health reasons

Twin Valley Farms, LLC   **Prattville, AL   1964–Present**

Managing Partner and Owner

PROFESSIONAL SOCIETIES
American Medical Association
American Board of Obstetrics and Gynecology, Diplomat
American College of Obstetrics and Gynecology, Fellow
American Fertility Society
Medical Association of the State of Alabama
Alabama Association of Obstetricians and Gynecologists
Jefferson County Medical Society
Greater Birmingham Obstetrical and Gynecological Society
Birmingham Clinical Club
Birmingham Surgical Society

HONORS
Alabama Healthcare Hall of Fame, inducted May 8, 2010

The Alfred Habeeb Distinguished Physicians Award, 2009
(St. Vincent's Hospital's highest medical staff award)

Physician Executive of the Year Award, 1996
(Medical Group Management Association and American College
of Medical Practice Executives)

American Medical Association, Member AMA Who's Who

University of Alabama in Birmingham, Birmingham, AL
• The Medical Center, University of Alabama Hospitals and Clinics
    • Elected Best Teaching Resident by Graduating Class of 1968
    • Intern and Resident Council, Member 1965–1968, President, 1967–1968
    • Best All Around Intern, 1962–1963

• University of Alabama Medical College of Alabama
    • Alpha Omega Alpha
    • Member, 1960–1962
    • President, 1961–1962

• University of Alabama
    • Alpha Epsilon Delta

PAST MEDICAL ACTIVITIES
Congress of the United States
• Appointed by the U.S. Congress to serve on the Physician Payment and
  Medical Technology Advisor Board, Office of Technology Assessment, 1985–1986

American Medical Association
• Member, 1963–Present
• House of Delegates, Member 1980–1987
• Council on Medical Service: Member, 1983–1987;
  Vice Chairman, 1986–1987
        • Chairman of the Council's Subcommittee on Financing Healthcare
            for the Elderly, 1984–1986
• Task Force on Physician Supply, Member 1985–1986

American College of Obstetricians and Gynecologists
• Task Force on Health Care Financing and Reimbursement, Chairman, 1984–1985

State of Alabama
• State Board of Medical Examiners, 1976–1982
• Board of Medical Scholarships Award, 1980–1984
• State Committee of Public Health, Member 1974–1981; Chairman of the
  Committee's Council on the Prevention of Disease and Medical Care, 1974–1975
• State Health Planning and Development Agency Board, 1974–1984

Medical Association of the State of Alabama
• Member, 1963–Present
• Board of Censors, 1976–1984
• President, 1982–1983
• Speaker, House of Delegates and College of Counselors, 1984–1986

Jefferson County Medical Society
• Member, 1968–Present
• Board of Trustees, 1972–1980
• Maternal and Child Health Committees, Chairman 1977–1981

St. Vincent's Hospital, Birmingham, Alabama
• Obstetrics and Gynecology Department, Member 1968–1994;
  Chairman 1970–1982
• Medical Staff, Member 1968–1994; President, 1989–1990
• Executive Committee, Member 1970–1992; Chairman 1975–1979

PAST COMMUNITY ACTIVITIES AND OTHER INTERESTS
Birmingham (Alabama) Area Chamber of Commerce, Member
Birmingham Steering Committee (Business/Medicine coalition), Member
Prattville (Alabama) Chamber of Commerce, Economic Development
  Committee, Member
Melaluca, Inc., Idaho Falls, Member, Board of Directors, 1998–2001
Myasthenia Gravis Foundation of America, Inc., Member, Board of Trustees, 2000

Myasthenia Gravis Foundation of America, Alabama Chapter
- Member, 1990–Present
- Board of Trustees, 1999–Present
- President, January 2001–January 2002

CURRENT COMMUNITY ACTIVITIES AND OTHER INTERESTS
President, Cross Creek Park Homeowner's Association, 2009–Present
Mountain Brook Baptist Church, Birmingham, AL, Deacon,
  Finance Committee Member
St. Vincent's Hospital Foundation, Birmingham, AL, Member,
  Board of Directors
The Rotary Club of Birmingham, Member
Mountain Brook Club, Member
The Club, Member
Newcomen Society, Member
Atlanta Cattlemen's Association, Member
Prattville (Alabama) YMCA, Member, Board of Directors, 1994–2001
Private Pilot, Instrument Rated

CURRENT PROFESSIONAL ACTIVITIES
University of Alabama School of Medicine at UAB, Clinical Professor
St. Vincent's Foundation, Birmingham, AL, Member
International Autoimmune Disease Research Foundation (IADRF),
  non-operational, Former Chairman
Twin Valley Farms, LLC, Prattville, AL, Managing Partner and Owner
Large single specialty practice consulting, 2004–Present
St. Vincent's Hospital Birmingham, coding coach, January 2011–2012
St. Vincent's Hospital Birmingham, utilization review consultant
  March 2012–Present (part-time)
The Cahaba Safeguard Administration, medical director, advising on abuse,
  over-use, and conditions of fraud, 1997–Present

BOOKS (as Author and/or as Publisher in role as Owner of Twin Valley Press)

Attacking Myasthenia Gravis (Subtitle: A Key in the Battle Against Autoimmune Disease), Ronald E. Henderson, M.D., Court Street Press, 2003.

The Woman I Am (Subtitle: A Woman's Guide to Health, Happiness, and Success in the 1990s), The Physicians of Henderson & Walton Women's Center, P.C., R. Henderson, P. Walton, F. Page, et al., as told to Anita Smith, Twin Valley Press, 1991.

Wadsworth Flats, Bill McDonald, Twin Valley Press, 1983.

APPENDIX B

What Makes Dr. Henderson Run?

William H. McDonald

"If by fate anyone means the will or power of God, let him keep his meaning but mend his language: for fate commonly means a necessary process which will have its way apart from the will of God and of men."

—St. Augustine, A.D. 427

Twelve days before Christmas 1974, Ronald E. Henderson, M.D., awoke in the ICU, not knowing how he got there or what was wrong with him.

He had no memory then, and has none today, of the exploding steel of the collision two days earlier, Dec. 11, at a dark and rainswept intersection as he sped to the hospital to answer a night emergency — third trimester bleeding in one of his patients.

What he does know he learned later: that the automobile that smashed into the left door of his little 240 Z sports car crushed his pelvis, fractured his femur in three places and came within an ace of ending the short, happy life of Ronald E. Henderson, M.D., at age 37.

He was not to leave the ICU until New Year's Eve, nor to leave the hospital until Jan. 16. Although he was to return to his busy Ob-Gyn practice a week after that, he did so by the grace of an Ironsides motorized wheelchair. For three months he delivered babies and performed surgery supported by a walker that had been draped in sterile linen at the scrub sink.

He was not to walk unassisted again until June.

Lying in the hospital, unable to turn, shave or comb his hair, he learned the meaning of total dependence for the first time in a life marked by uncommon independence. He learned the agony of waiting 30 minutes for a bed pan when he needed it then. He learned to reach out to those doctors and nurses whose empathy he felt. Not all had it.

Experiencing Helplessness

He had never missed a day from work or play in his life because of illness and thought he was some tough cookie. He learned the frailty and helplessness of illness and suffering. He learned the paramount importance of bedside nursing. Little things. Like placing water within easy reach. Back rubs. Clean sheets.

But most of all, empathy — the invisible radiations from those doctors and nurses who could identify with his predicament — not his illness so much as his *predicament*. Sympathy he could do without; he needed understanding.

The episode was an important turning point for Dr. Henderson — with all that time to read and think, understanding the truth of what Seneca meant when he wrote 2,000 years ago that "fate leads the willing, and drags along those who hang back."

The accident and his recovery from it solidified his belief in a concept that will be the theme of his 1982-83 MASA presidency — patient advocacy. It is preposterous, Dr. Henderson believes, that some hospitals have actually hired lay people called "Patient Advocates." Only the physician can perform that role, he believes, fearing that many have abdicated it.

The long, painful experience had other effects on him as well. What would he do with the rest of a life that had been spared?

"In a funny sort of way, it gave me confidence. Up until that time I thought I was tough. I knew that I was a little bit different from some people, and I hope that doesn't sound too egocentric.

"Now I know I can stand a challenge. This experience gave me confidence I didn't have, but thought I had. It took some of the brashness out of me. Not all of

continued on page 12

Above and right, Journal of the Medical Association of the State of Alabama, Vol. 51, No. 10, April, 1982. (continued from page 98)

it, maybe, but some of it. It was a humbling experience.

"I don't know all of how it affected me as an individual, because I am probably not objective enough to know. But of one thing I am certain: it changed my approach to the patient.

"I had always felt that the physician has to be the patient's advocate. Now I know it. It is something that most doctors don't understand: the patient has to have a spokesman. Only his doctor can fill that role. No one else has the training, no one else has the duty and responsibility. . . . "

Lost Concept

Patient advocacy is not a new concept, but a lost one, Dr. Henderson believes. It faded when doctors became too busy, when medicine became fractionalized. What once was second nature to physicians has now become a burden many of them shirk, he believes.

The trauma of a broken body had other effects on him that he finds difficulty even now articulating:

" . . . This happened at Christmastime . . . I had small children, 12, 10 and 7 at the time. . . . My wife was carrying home from the hospital A&P grocery sacks full of get-well cards. I remember I got 311 cards in one day. I had friends, physician friends, very busy, who would drive 100 miles to see me. . . .

" . . . It was a moving thing . . . I still get all choked up when I think about it. . . . "

The profoundly emotional experience thrust him into reflecting on his life, how and why it was spared, and what he intended to do with the balance of it. He developed time frames and flow charts lying there in the hospital. While he is not ready to reveal all of his decisions, he has gone public with one aspiration:

He has announced his decision to seek the presidency of the American Medical Association; he has given himself 12 years to achieve that objective.

Question: Is it prestige, glory, you seek, or what?

"I like to believe it's more than that, but it is that too. We all want recognition. I call it romance, in the largest sense. Romance can mean boy and girl, of course, and we all go through that. But romance can also mean wanting something very badly, achieving it and fulfilling that desire. Doing something well and knowing you are doing it well.

"You feel it, don't you? You're thinking how this will look in print when you shape and arrange it.

"If my mother and father taught me one thing well, back on the 116-acre farm in Autauga County that I grew up on, it was this: Whatever you do, always do your best. No matter what it is, make it the best. They hammered that into me, and I have tried to live by it."

Question: All right, then, Dr. Henderson, it is the year 1995, or thereabouts. You have achieved your objective as president of AMA, a heady experience. But now your term is over. You have returned to Birmingham. Is that all? What now?

Sitting there in his comfortable office, tastefully appointed in what can best be described as Americanized Oriental, or Orientalized American, he fingers the collar of his scrub suit, looks at the remains of his lunch on his desk, moves the empty Sun-Maid raisin box a tad while he marshals his thoughts, and begins talking again, slowly at first, then picking up speed. You know by now what follows will be preface to a position statement:

"I was coming back from a Reference Committee F meeting with the AMA Board of Trustees in Chicago. [He is chairman of that committee this year.] Over North Tennessee we hit a thunderstorm. It was throwing that 727 around everywhere all over the sky. And I wondered: What in the hell am I doing here? I could be home in my easy chair with my paper, with my slippers on . . . !

"Sometimes I do wonder what I'm doing but most of the time I think I have a real sense, a calling, to repay what society has done for me.

"As you know, I came from a rural background — solid, salt-of-the-earth people. Before me there was one cousin, on both sides of the family, that had a college education. One cousin. Then my brothers that followed, and some later.

"All of them gave me a leg up. I stood on their shoulders. I have been very fortunate and I have a deep need to pay some civic rent. And that's not just [expletive deleted]. I really want to have an impact. I want to give something back to society. . . . "

Question: But you have already, haven't you? And back to the question, what happens in 1995, assuming that objective has been achieved. Most people would see the presidency of AMA as a terminal ambition for a physician. Obviously you don't see it that way. It's not just the glory you want, but the chance to be of service, to get your message across to a larger audience. Then what?

"I am not sure yet. I think something out there is much different and much bigger than the presidency of the AMA for me. Whether it involves public service, a management job somewhere, I don't know. . . . "

An Eye On Washington?

Question: You mentioned public service. Might that involve national affairs, politics, Congress, the United States Senate? You don't rule out any of these?

Dr. Henderson shakes his head slowly. The raisin box requires his undivided attention for a moment. Then:

"I think there is a real need for professions other than law at the national level — farmers, businessmen, doctors.

"I think it's time the pendulum swings back away from the law and that some of the other professions — and businessmen and farmers — become involved. Think of all the doctors who signed the Declaration of

Independence; of all the farmers who helped found the Republic.

"It is difficult of course for a professional man to make the transition, the sacrifice, because it's not a lateral move. In compensation and time commitment, it is definitely not a lateral move. . . . "

But the light in his eye is not illumined by that empty Sun-Maid box. It's a familiar light to one who has spent a professional lifetime observing its flicker in men who feel they have been tapped by destiny to lead, to carry their message, to fight for their convictions, to enter their ideas in the open lists and stand or fall on their merit.

Ron Henderson first saw the light of day on July 28, 1937 in Prattville, Alabama. His father and mother brought him up under strict rules of personal accountability. They urged him, as did his friends and teachers, to enter one of the professions, but it was not until the 11th grade that he was sure he wanted to be a physician.

His parents were pleased. His father had been in the top of his Sidney Lanier High School (Montgomery) graduating class of 1929 but could not afford college.

"This was a generational tragedy," Dr. Henderson recalls. "He graduated the year of the stock market crash and many like him had no hope of higher education."

They worked to provide hope for the next generation.

Dr. Newton, Benefactor

Money was still short. Ron Henderson had to borrow and work at summer jobs to make his way through college and medical school. One summer he came home without any prospect of work and stopped by the office of the kindly, respected physician who had been his inspiration, Dr. George Newton. Before even going home, Henderson carried his suitcase to Dr. Newton's office and asked to see the doctor. He wanted a job.

Dr. Newton saw him immediately, picked up the phone, made one phone call and Ron Henderson had a summer job at Continental Gin, on the 3 to 11 shift.

His role model, early and late, was Dr. Newton, who had begun to be an encouragement about the time Henderson began playing end on the Autauga County High School football team.

Winning his B.S. in 1958 and his M.D. in 1962, Dr. Henderson went on to be tapped Outstanding Intern in 1963.

In fulfillment of his state scholarship obligation, and because he still wanted to emulate Dr. Newton, he spent two years, 1963-65, in general practice in Gordo.

But he had been brainwashed, as he puts it, while in medical school and longed to return for specialty training in obstetrics and gynecology. He had been inspired while on this rotation by two residents who loved what they were doing and were intensely interested in patient care.

"You get brainwashed in the first two years," Dr. Henderson recalls, "and when you hit the clinics you are really set up to go into some specialty. I think it's still that way; it hasn't changed a bit. You are brainwashed into believing you can't practice in a rural setting, that you have got to have the mecca, all that sophisticated equipment and technology, to survive.

"I was prone to that. . . . "

He was also prone to hard work and dedication. The graduating class of 1968 named him Best Resident.

Farewell to Tuscaloosa

He had planned to return to Tuscaloosa to practice, having contracted that community's famed village virus, but received an irresistible offer from St. Vincent's Hospital in Birmingham. He has practiced there since 1968.

Early on, earning his niche in medicine, the attendant rewards in remuneration and recognition were important goals. Now he is elevating his sights to other life objectives according to plans crystallized during his hospital stay.

Although he is still fascinated by the romance of his work, he has set for himself new mountains to climb, thus to keep the creative juices flowing.

"If I fall off the ladder, if I can't reach another rung, I'll bail out.

"I realize I have a lot of growing to do. I have a lot of learning ahead of me. I will get into some fights and probably get bloodied. But I don't see many people without stature who have achieved the presidency of AMA. They are tough but compassionate, with a lot of ability. I may not have it, but I'm going to give it a shot.

"I feel that my diverse background — rural rearing, state university, exposure to rural health again as a general practitioner, and my specialty practice in an urban area — gives me an opportunity that other people don't have.

"I have had tremendous support around the state. Members of the Board of Censors have encouraged me. Dean Pittman [James A. Pittman, Jr., M.D., Executive Dean, UAB School of Medicine] has given me a lot of support."

Dean Pittman nominated Dr. Henderson for the MASA presidency at annual session in Mobile last year. While he was at it, he tacked on the nomination for the AMA presidency. That was out of order but definitely in harmony. The Dean says:

"Ron Henderson has been an outstanding person since he was in medical school. He has seen medicine from the 'real doctor' point of view in his general practice in Gordo. He is a highly respected specialist now in Birmingham.

"He has seen medicine from the consumer point of view in his traumatic automobile accident. He knows, as well as anyone I can think of, what medicine is and what it ought to be. I support him 100%. . . . "

14 / Journal of the Medical Association of the State of Alabama

Above and right, Journal of the Medical Association of the State of Alabama, Vol. 51, No. 10, April, 1982.
(continued from page 98)

Where It Began

In grammar school, something happened that may have been a factor in Dr. Henderson's parallel interests in farming and public service. He entered an essay in a county-wide contest on What It Means To Be An American. He won a Yorkshire gilt (a female pig) for his effort, convincing him that: (1) He always wanted to keep his hand in farming; and (2) he could achieve the heights if he wanted to.

The family farm had been mainly devoted to row-cropping, but Dr. Henderson thought the greater Romance (the operative word for him) lay in cattle farming.

In 1963-64 he bought a half-interest in the old home place from his Dad, cleared the land and began thinking cattle. He bought his present 1,600-acre spread in 1970 a few miles from the old home place.

Twin Valley Farms, as a sign prominently proclaims it, is presently home for about 500 head of commercial cattle and 60 registered cattle, Angus and Hereford, and bulls.

The population includes one that may be the wave of the future: an embryonic transplant. Dr. Henderson:

"I feel it is the quickest way to get a superior herd without costing an arm and a leg."

Transplant, now being done widely, enables the cattleman to leapfrog several generations in his breeding work. The embryo may be transplanted immediately to the donor cow or frozen for later use.

"They are doing cloning now," Dr. Henderson says, "getting three individuals exactly alike genetically. They take the embryo in the early stages, split it and then, because of time, split it again so that they end up with three individuals of the same genetics. Conception rate is about 17%, which is pretty good.

"Veterinary science is far ahead of human reproduction. But they don't have to worry about religion and morals and other hang-ups."

Theme for 1982-83

As MASA President he hopes to have an impact in an area dear to his heart since the earliest days of training but intensified and given shape by his automobile accident — patient advocacy.

"I want physicians of the state to realize and to remember that they are the patient's advocate. The Medical Association is a perfect place for such an attitude to be promoted. It's not only the way it *ought* to be: it's the way it's *got* to be.

"We've got to get away from the idea that the attending physician does not always perceive himself as the primary care physician — with the result that the patient really doesn't have an advocate.

"Also I want to educate the physicians of this state about what is happening in our society affecting medical care. Most physicians are not aware, I'm afraid, of

continued on page 17

Dr. Henderson
continued from page 14

all the changes taking place — changes that, in the next five years, will alter the total landscape of medicine as we have known it in the past. So many pressures coming from so many sources make change inevitable. And it's right ahead of us. I want to be an instrument of educating physicians to these changes."

Physicians are so busy these days, Dr. Henderson continued, they have not taken time to see what is happening to change medicine radically:

"For instance, industry's push to get a handle on costs. We have the highest quality of medical care the world has ever seen for any population. It's accessible to a higher percentage of patients than ever before.

"We've done so well, the cost is out of hand. If we don't get better control of costs, if we don't contain costs, I believe this failure is going to tear down the whole system.

"We have industry wanting change, unions saying that too much of their take-home dollar goes to fringe benefits; we have insurance companies saying they can't sell insurance because the cost is prohibitive.

"I think physicians should take the lead. They're the ones who *must* take the lead. I think that because of the entry into the health care system of the for-profit corporations, competition has gotten so intense among hospitals they don't have a long-term view.

"They spent $1.2 million on CON applications alone just in Jefferson County last year. That's passed on to the patient.

"Physicians have got to be willing to look at alternative methods of health care: outpatient surgery, outpatient diagnostic procedures, promotion of good health — exercise, no smoking, weight control, the whole bit.

"If we can achieve these things, we can salvage some part of the free practice of medicine. If we don't, it's going to change. You have the pressures to contain costs at the same time we are facing a doctor surplus. With those two factors in the equation, something is going to happen.

"Maybe when this competition begins to hurt, more doctors will be interested in salvaging the free practice of medicine."

Keep Moving On

Dr. Henderson is a restless and impatient man at times, reflected in his compulsion to get up and walk around when meetings drag on.

That he is driven, he freely admits. And he has expressed some concern for the bellicose scowl that descends over his face at times, even when he may be thinking the most placid thoughts.

The root of that dark and malevolent visage could be the small, insistent voice inside that keeps admonishing him to stop all this shilly-shallying and get on with the life plan.   ▣

ONE ON ONE

Henderson sees health care becoming centralized

"Ob/gyn? It's the most exciting, fulfilling field. I wouldn't want to do anything else. My work is so very rewarding and I look forward to it every day."

Ronald E. Henderson, M.D., was born in Prattville, attended the University of Alabama and went to medical school at the Medical College of Alabama. He did his internship and residency at University of Alabama Hospitals and Clinics.

While specializing in gynecology, obstetrics, and infertility, Henderson emphasizes preventive medicine and the long-term beneficial effects of a healthy lifestyle. He has been putting these prin-

present and it makes me think of the unique way the Chinese write the word "crisis". It's a combination of the two words "danger" and "opportunity". It's an opportunity for those willing to take risks.

AHN: HOW HAS THIS PARTICULAR SERVICE CHANGED THE MOST?

HENDERSON: It's incredibly different from when I started 20 years ago. We didn't have ultrasound, amniocentesis, fetal monitoring, sigmoidoscopy, except experimentally. It's a more comfortable

on call for obstetrical patients and we have plans for a third team. Also, we've enlarged our geographic service to Cullman, Sylacauga and Anniston for prenatal care and to see gynecology patients. Also, we have applied for national standards for health screenings and cancer screenings. If a patient is overweight, we suggest they see our nutritionist. If a patient is a smoker, we suggest they go to smoking cessation classes. We want to make this a one-stop shopping place. We offer primary care, specialty care and care for minor health problems.

And the most exciting thing about our

rather keep people from getting in trouble. Preventive medicine.

AHN: DO YOU BELIEVE MOST DOCTORS STRESS PREVENTIVE MEDICINE?

HENDERSON: Certainly not enough. For example, we have cardiovascular surgeons who put people through extensive, dangerous surgery and send them out without telling them what kind of diet they should be on. They don't always send them to a nutritionist for the very important information they need. There's inadequate follow-up with that surgeon regarding their patients.

And some doctors don't practice preventive medicine personally, and to me, that is very hypocritical. Approximately 30 percent of doctors still smoke. Now, for a physician to sit and smoke and tell his patients that smoking is an unhealthy thing to do, well, that's not being a very good role model. The same applies to the doctors who are obese. They tell their patients to lose weight. The way they look speaks louder than what they are saying and I think it affects their credibility. If they're going to set an example, let it be a positive one.

"BMC's costs far exceeded other hospitals we do business with. It seems to me their cost structure has gotten out of line."

*Ron Henderson, M.D.
Founder, Chairman of the Board
Southeast Health Plan*

ciples into practice for more than 20 years and has incorporated them into what has become Henderson and Walton Women's Center.

Henderson is founder, president and Chairman of the Board of Southeast Health Plan, Inc., is currently serving as a member of the House of Delegates of the American Medical Association and has previously served as a member of the AMA's Council on Medical Service. He is a past president of the State Medical Association of Alabama, served as Chief of Obstetrics and Gynecology at St. Vincent's Hospital for 12 years and is Clinical Professor in the University of Alabama at Birmingham School of Medicine Department of Obstetrics and Gynecology.

He is married and has three children.

AHN: HOW WOULD YOU DESCRIBE THE PRACTICE OF OB/GYN IN 1988?

HENDERSON: Well, I've been in practice for 20 years and you can't refute the facts of escalating liability premiums and the indigent care situation. We're also facing the costs of paying nurses, overhead, insurance, equipment—and yet, this is the most exciting, fulfilling field to be in. We're not crying, "Woe is me." It's a diverse specialty and we provide primary care and we can get as specialized as we want. Also, there are so many subspecialties. The liability thing is ever

specialty now. We can do more for the patient than we ever could before. Technology notwithstanding, there is still going to be some poor outcomes. For example, the malpractice lawyers focus on the time the patient is under the direct care of the physician only. The real issue often times is what happens when the patient is at home. We insist on proper diet, exercise, no smoking, not taking any drugs not prescribed by us. And most of the time our patients comply. But, those who don't sometimes run into physical problems.

The most regrettable thing that has happened in the medical field is the professional liability bear. This thing has drawn a barrier between the physician and the patient. Every patient is a potential adversary. I say to my people, "We're going to show compassion to our patients and explain things to our patients. We're going to maintain a rapport with our patients". It's very human for doctors to withdraw behind technology and not get close to their patients. I feel privileged to be a physician. I believe it's an honor. I don't like a lot of things that are happening, but I'm going to enjoy the practice of medicine for as long as I can.

AHN: WHAT ARE SOME INNOVATIVE ASPECTS OF YOUR PRACTICE?

HENDERSON: I think we've done some exciting things. We have two teams

practice is the infertility services we can now provide.

AHN: YOU REALLY FEEL STRONGLY ABOUT PREVENTIVE HEALTH MANAGEMENT, DON'T YOU?

HENDERSON: Definitely! There's an anecdote that illustrates how I feel about preventive health care. A cardiovascular surgeon and a physiologist were out fishing at a small lake. They looked across the lake and saw a man struggling for help. He was yelling, "Help me. I'm drowning. Help me!" The two doctors ran to the man and pulled him out. They came back to their fishing spot and continued reeling in the fish. The second time they heard another yell from across the lake. Another man was in trouble. "Come on," said the cardiovascular man, "let's go save this one, too." Off they ran and pulled the second man out of the water.

They returned to their fishing when they heard, for the third time, cries for help from across the lake. "O.K.," said the cardiovascular man, "let's go save this one." The physiologist didn't budge, and stood with arms folded. "Come on," insisted his friend, "let's go save this third man."

"Not this time," said the physiologist. "We need to decide *why* they're getting in trouble."

It's my feeling that we physicians need to be the physiologists. I'd much

AHN: WHERE DO YOU SEE MEDICINE HEADING IN THE FUTURE?

HENDERSON: I see obstetrics leading the way to centralization of acute medical care. Also, I think rural hospitals will go out of business. Obstetrics will get more and more sophisticated and not every hospital will be able to afford the equipment. In addition, I see two or three large programs in the major cities. I don't believe the smaller hospitals will survive.

AHN: HOW DID SOUTHEAST HEALTH PLAN COME ABOUT?

HENDERSON: In 1983, I saw in Alabama, no real alternative to the third party payors. So, I got a group of physicians together and we formed a for-profit plan. Currently, we have 35,000 members enrolled with Southeast. This includes Birmingham, Mobile, Tuscaloosa and contiguous counties.

AHN: THERE HAS BEEN TALK THAT THE BAPTIST MEDICAL CENTERS WILL NO LONGER BE PART OF THE SOUTHEAST HEALTH PLAN. CAN YOU EXPLAIN WHY?

HENDERSON: We operate or S
continued next page

The Prattville Progress, September 1988. *(continued from page 117)*

leum Company. He is responsible for directing the division's general purchasing, fleet purchasing and logistics for surface transportation. He lives in Ona, W.Va.

64 **Dorothy G. Grimes** has been named chairwoman of the University of Montevallo's English Department.

65 Bowling Green, Ky., resident **James D. Harris**, JD '67, has been appointed to the Kentucky Continuing Legal Education.

66 **James M. Marriner** is serving as general manager-comptrollers for BellSouth Telecommunications operations in Louisiana and Mississippi. He has been elected president of the New Orleans chapter of the Financial Executives Institute.

67 The Honorable **Joseph A. Colquitt**, JD '70, former presiding judge of Alabama's Sixth Judicial Circuit, recently received the American Judicature Society's Herbert Harley Award in recognition of his contributions to improving the administration of justice in Alabama. Colquitt is currently professor of law and director of trial advocacy programs at The University of Alabama School of Law.

69 Eastern Kentucky University dean of the College of Education **Kenneth T. Henson** is co-author of Macmillan Publishers' introductory education text, *Education: An Introduction*, 4th ed. Henson is author of 13 books and more than 100 articles in professional journals.

Jane Hardwick Riley has been appointed principal of Thompson Middle School in Alabaster, Ala.

71 Jackson, Miss., resident **Ann Williams** recently received an American Society of Interior Designers Medalists Award. The Medalists Award is the highest chapter award bestowed by the society to a member. Williams is owner of Alice Ann Interiors.

72 ITT Consumer Financial Corporation has named **Robert H. Carpenter Jr.**, JD '75, to the position of general counsel and senior vice president in the company's Plymouth, Minn., home offices. Carpenter joins the company from Household International, where he served as general counsel and vice president of its U.S. consumer and mortgage banking businesses.

Charlie S. McAdams has been pro-

As for his interest in agriculture, his Twin Valley Farms operation, which covers more than 1,800 acres, registered 250 Angus cattle with the American Angus Association in 1992—the most by any Alabama Angus breeder. By the end of calving season in May, the farmer-turned-doctor may have more than 300 registered Angus.

Agriculture, says Henderson, is the spark that fueled his success in both the medical profession and the cattle industry. As a young boy, he was active in local 4-H and FFA clubs. At age 8, the farm boy entered a countywide essay contest that changed his life. His subject? "What it means to be an American."

"It was one of the most meaningful things that has ever happened to me," Henderson says. "For the first time in my life I realized that I could be competitive in the larger sense."

Although he expressed an early desire to pursue a career in agriculture, another occupation caught Henderson's eye— medicine. His interest grew largely from the boyhood admiration he developed for his hometown doctor, George Newton.

"Dr. Newton was a caring man and full of energy," Henderson remembers, adding that the general practitioner frequently made visits to their household to care for his ailing grandmother. "Fortunately, Dr. Newton took an interest in me and would take me with him on housecalls. Before I finished high school I had developed an intense desire to study medicine."

But studying medicine meant going to college, something no one in Henderson's immediate family had ever done. "We came from a rural background," he explained. "College was not really an option."

When folks in Henderson's hometown learned of his passion for medicine, sending the Autauga County High School three-sports star to college soon became a community project. "It was incredible," he says. "It seemed like everyone in the community helped me in different ways, from voicing encouragement to providing me with after-school and summer jobs."

Upon graduation, Henderson hitch-

Dr. Ron Henderson

hiked his way to Tuscaloosa to study biology and physics. He says, "It hit me when I walked onto The University of Alabama campus in 1955, that even though I came from a rural school and that I was competing with people from all across the country, I was no different than anybody else. I realized immediately that I had the same opportunities to succeed as any other student."

Henderson fondly recalls, "When I was in school, professors took an interest in freshmen and would follow you through college as an adviser, friend and confidant. You could come from any background and if you were willing to work hard and mind your Ps and Qs, you could be successful."

In 1959 he received a bachelor's degree in physics. He went on to The University of Alabama's school of medicine in Birmingham where he finished in 1962. After completing a medical residency program in Birmingham, he moved to west Alabama and worked for two years as a general practitioner in Gordo. In 1965 he moved back to Birmingham to complete his final three-year residency training, and, in 1968, at age 30, he began his gynecology and obstetrics practice, which later became Henderson & Walton Women's Center.

Even as he prepared for a medical career, Henderson never lost touch with his roots. In 1964 he bought half interest in his family's 116-acre homeplace in Autauga County and soon purchased 30 Polled Herefords and an Angus bull. In 1970 he expanded his cattle operation and purchased a farm near Prattville, which today is home to Twin Valley Farms.

In retrospect, Henderson credits his on-and-off-the-farm success to his longtime romance with medicine and agriculture. The physician-cattleman insists that folks must pursue careers that they love. "It's simple," he says, "If you don't love your work you won't be successful."

By Mark Morrison, '86, publications director for the Alabama Farmers Federation and former Alumni Magazine assistant editor

Alabama Alumni, University of Alabama magazine, December 1992. *(continued from page 129)*

lifestyle. Based at St. Vincent's Hospital in Birmingham, Henderson & Walton Women's Center is one of the largest and most unique private practices of its kind in the country. The practice also has satellite offices in Alabaster, Anniston, Cullman, Jasper, Sylacauga and Tuscaloosa. In 1993, a Henderson & Walton Women's Center is scheduled to open in Atlanta.

AGRICULTURE, SAYS HENDERSON, IS THE spark that fueled his success in both the cattle business and the medical profession. As a youngster, he was always active in local 4-H and FFA clubs. At age 8, the young farm boy entered a countywide essay contest that literally changed his life. His subject? "What it means to be an American."

"It was one of the most meaningful things that has ever happened to me," Henderson says. "I was one of six essay winners."

His prize? A Yorkshire gilt.

"My responsibility as a contest winner was to help expand the herd. In two years I gave two gilts back to the program," he says.

Winning the essay competition was a turning point in Henderson's life. He says, "For the first time in my life I realized that I could be competitive in the larger since."

Although he expressed an early desire to pursue agriculture full time, another occupation caught Henderson's eye—medicine. He says his interest in becoming a physician grew largely from his admiration of the "town doctor" and the delicate skills it took to be a general family practitioner. Before he finished high school, he had developed an intense desire to study medicine.

Henderson's passion for medicine led him to The University of Alabama after high school. He studied biology and physics and received his bachelor's degree in 1959. He went on to The University of Alabama's School of Medicine in Birmingham where he finished in 1962. After completing a medical residency program in Birmingham, Henderson moved to west Alabama and worked for three years as a general practitioner in Gordo. In 1965 he moved back to Birmingham to complete his final three-year residency training, and, in 1968, at age 30, he began his gynecology and obstetrics practice, which later became Henderson & Walton Women's Center.

EVEN AS HE PREPARED FOR A career in medicine, Henderson never lost touch with his rural roots. In 1964 he bought a half interest in his family's 116-acre Autauga County homeplace and soon purchased 30 Polled Herefords and an Angus bull. In 1970 he purchased the Ward farm on Autauga County Road 41 near Prattville, which, today, is home to Twin Valley Farms.

In the late '70s, feeling that his Twin Valley cattle operation was less successful than it should be, Henderson turned to his long-time friend and farm mentor, Ed Wadsworth, for guidance.

The rest, says Henderson, is history.

Henderson's goal as a physician is to deliver the highest quality medical care possible to women.

Henderson sold his commercial herd and went into the purebred business. In 1989, Twin Valley developed a three-year goal to become the dominate Angus herd—not just in Alabama, but in the Southeast. "We're almost there," he says.

Among its peers, Twin Valley Farms has become a leading source of predictable performance genetics in Alabama. Its bulls are consistently top performers in annual Beef Cattle Improvement Association (BCIA) bull tests around the state. And Twin Valley sells more bulls to commercial cattlemen than any other breeder in the Southeast.

WITH A BUSY MEDICAL PRACTICE in Birmingham, Henderson spends as much time at Twin Valley Farms as his hectic schedule permits. He resents, however, being called just a "doctor farmer."

"I don't consider myself a typical 'gentleman farmer,' " he explains. "I know cattle raising from the ground up. I didn't get into this as a hobby."

Twin Valley Farms has a staff of six full-time and two part-time employees, and usually employs two agricultural interns. Buddy McDaniel, who has been with Twin Valley for almost 10 years, is the farm's manager and Roland Starnes has recently joined the Angus operation as cattle manager.

"Our goal is to build a 400-head brood cow herd," says Henderson. "We will have about 310 calves this year. We will have about 40 bulls in our upcoming fall bull sale scheduled for Nov. 7. Next year we will have 80 bulls for sale, building toward a goal of having 100 bulls for sale each fall."

"The demand for Angus genetics has never been greater than it is today," says Henderson, who has striven for years to offer new genetics and leadership to the beef industry.

Part of the demand for improving the breed, says Henderson, is the consumer's demand for leaner beef products—a demand which the physician fully understands and appreciates.

"We are interested at Twin Valley in being a leader in developing lean, low-fat beef," says Henderson. "The problem with beef is that it is so darn good, and so tasty, that people eat too much of it. With the lean approach and a balanced diet, beef is a very healthy food source."

FOR HENDERSON, AND HIS WIFE, BETH, also a Prattville native, Twin Valley Farms has come a long way. "Twin Valley began with the end in mind, and we've been whittling on it for more than 20 years," says Henderson.

"I hope when people think of Twin Valley, they'll think of it as a fun place that operates on Christian principles...and raises the best Angus you can buy." ∎

Neighbors, Alfa magazine, October 1992. *(continued from page 131)*

Henderson rides herd on Twin Valley

By Barbara Knight
The Prattville Progress

Dr. Ron Henderson, owner of Twin Valley Farms near Prattville spent his formative years on his family's Autauga County cotton, corn and cattle farm.

Today Henderson is one of the most successful Angus beef cattle breeders in the country. He has also been a leader in women's health care. He specializes in gynecology, obstetrics and infertility at Birmingham's Henderson, Walton Women's Center (now Medisphere Health Partners), one of the largest and most unique private practices of its kind in the country. The center has satellite offices in seven central Alabama towns.

Henderson also founded a Birmingham-based physicians practice management company that has a national focus.

"I'm the luckiest guy in the world," he said. "My work is my hobby. I love medicine. I love people. And I have a tremendous love for agriculture, particularly

Lisa Bundy/Staff

Dr. Ron Henderson looks over some of the herd at his Twin Valley Farms in Autauga County. It's one of the nation's foremost Angus cattle operations.

farming. I have been able to combine all these things."

Henderson's knowledge has served to develop a premiere operation in Autauga County

that could serve as a "poster child" for modern farming. The farm's 3,000 owned and leased acres are home to 1,400 head of cattle.

In 1964 Henderson bought half-interest in his family's 116-acre home-place farm. He purchased the Ward Farm on

(Please see FARM,page 2)

Farm

(Continued from page 1)
Autauga County Road 41 in 1970. At that time, the farm had a commercial herd consisting of 100 cows and 25 heifers. Henderson combined his two herds and several years later renamed his enterprise Twin Valley Farms.

When the cattle operation failed to live up to his expectations, Henderson sought the advice of his long-time friends Buzz Wendland and the late Edward Wadsworth.

The commercial herd was phased out in 1983 and by 1989 Twin Valley entered the purebred business. The farm's national reputation is spread through the organization's two major sales held each year.

Wendland, also a successful Autauga County farmer and businessman, praised Hender-

son's operation.

"Twin Valley Farms is a tremendous asset to our community," he said. "Dr. Ron Henderson and his management team, headed by Roland Starnes, have a breeding and management program that is nationally recognized. Their vision and enthusiasm make them and their cattle truly leaders in the industry."

Henderson's wife Beth is an Autauga native.

During the past fall and spring calving season Twin Valley Farms produced 500 calves. Henderson predicts that number will escalate to 550 by next year.

The calves are products of both natural breeding and artificial insemination.

"Artificial insemination is certainly more expensive to do," Henderson explained, "but the

upside of artificial insemination is that we can hormonally treat a valuable cow and cause it to produce more than one egg pre cycle."

The treated cow can produce up to 35 embryos in one cycle. The embryos are removed every 90 days and placed in surrogate mother cows.

"This method allows us to comfortably invest our money (in quality stock) because we know we can recover our investment on that money," he said. "For example, at one time we had 27 calves from one cow and her daughter and the same bull. The calves were either full brother and sisters or three-quarter brothers and sisters genetically."

Henderson said his goal is to improve the food supply to a rapidly over-populated globe. "One

very good way to do that is to convert grass to beef," he said.

His earliest and perhaps most influential role model was his father, William Earl Henderson, who died in 1987.

"He as the hardest working man I've ever known," said Henderson.

In the past, Henderson has divided his time between his medical practice and Twin Valley. He plans to spend more time on his farming enterprise.

Twin Valley will hold its 13th annual Angus Spirit Production Sale starting at noon Saturday. The sale is expected to attract buyers from across the nation.

For more information on the sale, call Roland Starnes, general manager, at 365-9966.

The Prattville Progress, 1997. (continued from page 149)

Looking for a cure

Myasthenia gravis victim seeks research funds

By **KATHERINE BOUMA**
News staff writer

When Dr. Ron Henderson began to suffer the first signs of a neurological disease in the hot summer of 1994, he knew it wasn't stress.

"I've always thrived on having three or four balls in the air at one time," he said.

At the time, the 56-year-old was maintaining a medical practice, acting as CEO of a physicians management company and running a cattle ranch. During his career, he had started three other companies and served as president of the Medical Association of the State of Alabama.

When he reported to his doctor with exhaustion and muscle twitches, he found himself on the other side of the desk. Like 60 percent of women and 40 percent of men ultimately diagnosed with myasthenia gravis, he was referred to a psychiatrist.

Henderson didn't take his doctor's recommendation. Nor did he follow his own instinct to make an appointment with a neurologist.

Instead, as his symptoms worsened, Henderson incorrectly self-diagnosed ALS, the incurable and rapidly degenerative disease of the nervous system commonly called Lou Gehrig's disease.

He was forced to give up his exercise regimen because he didn't have the strength.

He retired from his medical practice at Henderson-Walton Women's Center. He kept working as CEO of MediSphere Corp., but he dramatically changed his schedule. Every 90-minute meeting required a 90-minute nap.

"If I didn't really concentrate, my head would flop back in meetings," he said.

In December of 1995, when he lost the ability to chew his own food, Henderson said he told his wife, Beth, he had bad news and good news.

The new symptom meant his disease was progressive. But it also allowed him to rule out ALS. He went to a neurologist and was diagnosed with myasthenia gravis.

Unlike ALS, myasthenia gravis can be treated, although it is not curable.

It's taken Henderson years to come to terms with his disease and find a suitable regimen of medicines. But he now believes his terminal diagnosis gave him a greater purpose in life.

He said he is working to raise funds for

► See **Disease**, Page 2D

> *"It would open up a floodgate for a cure for hundreds of thousands of people. When I practiced medicine I did one patient at a time. If this does work — gosh, the ramifications of that."*
>
> **Dr. Ron Henderson**
> *who is working to raise funds for research on several rare autoimmune diseases*

DISEASE:

Vaccine shows promise in animals

► From Page **1D**

research that may lead to cures for asthma, lupus, rheumatoid arthritis, certain types of diabetes and other rare autoimmune diseases.

"It would open up a floodgate for a cure for hundreds of thousands of people," he said. "When I practiced medicine I did one patient at a time. If this does work — gosh, the ramifications of that."

In myasthenia gravis, the patient's immune system attacks the receptors that cause muscles to contract, said J. Edwin Blalock, a professor of physiology and biophysics at the University of Alabama School of Medicine in Birmingham.

"It impairs the ability of the muscle to receive information from the nerve," Blalock said.

As a result, the muscles fatigue extremely quickly after minor exercise or exertion.

"Through the course of the day, they sort of get weaker and weaker and weaker," he said.

Most patients turn up at a doctor's office when their eyelids quit functioning properly, he said. Henderson has no trouble with his eyelids, he said, which may be one reason his diagnosis initially confounded him and his physician.

But the muscles of his forehead sagged so much that last year he needed to have plastic surgery so that he could see under his own brow, Henderson said.

Myasthenia gravis patients can die of respiratory failure when the muscles controlling the diaphragm fail.

"People with MG can have a propensity to choke while they're eating," Blalock said. "It's a very scary disease if you have it. I think the medical establishment's view is that it's a manageable disease. If you ask any myasthenic, the problem is the quality of life is not very good."

It's not known what causes the disease, Blalock said. There is a weak genetic link, but experts believe there must also be an environmental factor.

Fewer than 40,000 people in the United States are known to be afflicted with the disease, which usually strikes women in their 20s or 30s and men in their 50s or 60s.

But a cure for MG could affect many more people, Blalock said.

He began research on MG in an effort to find a cure for autoimmune diseases. He looked for a disease that is similar in animals and humans, since he'd have to start testing on animals.

Blalock has developed an immunization that causes the body to make a second antibody to attack the antibodies that cause MG.

He hopes a human vaccine can be developed, although he says that will require about $3.5 million. If a vaccine can be created that cures MG in humans, there's no reason vaccines for other autoimmune diseases couldn't be developed the same way, Blalock said.

So far, Blalock's vaccine has prevented and cured the disease in laboratory rats and pet dogs. Blalock said it's unclear whether the animals have any lingering damage from their bouts with MG.

"I can tell you anecdotally what the people with these dogs tell me, which is that their dogs are happier and their quality of life is better," he said. "They no longer require medications in order to function."

Henderson also is functioning better than he was a few years ago.

"I can work out. I can open a bottle," he said. "I have a lot more strength than in my darkest days. I'm so much better I'm almost euphoric."

However, he said he understands that the disease is cyclic and that the effects of medicines he is feeling right now may not last forever. "I want to live as long as I can, but I'm at peace with leaving this life."

To contact the Alabama Chapter of the Myasthenia Gravis Foundation of America, call 205-868-1210 or go to *http://homepages.msn.com/SupportSt/mgalabama/*

The Birmingham News, November 2001. *(continued from page 149)*

HENDERSON:
Book's proceeds to help foundation

From Page 1E

Today, though, he wants to bring attention to autoimmune disorders and the challenges of the people who live with chronic illness and whose who take care of them.

After a 1994 retirement party that seemed more like a wake than celebration, Henderson exiled himself to his Prattville farm. He was taking steroids, which changed his trim appearance and made his behavior erratic. He was unhappy and felt disconnected.

He expected to die from the ravages of the disease, in which muscles don't receive impulses from the nerve. MG patients fatigue quickly and muscles begin to atrophy without normal use. Many MG patients die because they can no longer breathe effectively.

Henderson's story is pretty typical of anyone with a serious chronic illness, he says. They often fold up their tents, isolate themselves from family and friends, and wait for all the symptoms and the death that will send them to the grave.

It doesn't have to be that way, says Henderson, whose disease went into remission. With diet, exercise, smart rest periods and social outlets, he not only began to take control of his disease and life but also to realize that many others were fighting back just as he was.

His book tells his story and that of three other MG patients — Pastor Steve Gaines of First Baptist Church of Gardendale; family physician Steve TePastte of Holt, Mich.; and public relations rep Kelley Haughey of Wayne, N.J.

TePastte, who went from healthy to a ventilator-supported existence in hours, blames his decision to take echinacea because he was feeling poorly after a series of viruses. He believes that herbal supplement overstimulated his al-

NEWS STAFF/BEVERLY TAYLOR

Take charge of your illness, Ron Henderson advises patients with chronic illnesses such as his myasthenia gravis.

ready-stressed immune system and led to a rapid decline.

His favorite part of Henderson's book, TePastte says, is Henderson's admonition to physicians to allow patients to take control of their illness, and to act as advisers and partners rather than dictators.

Haughey agrees.

"You're the one who has to live with it," she says. "If your doctor doesn't know any new treatments, and there are new treatments, I suggest you get up and get out and find a new doctor. Don't worry about hurting anyone's feelings."

Bridging gaps

Henderson's three-pronged plan of attack — book, foundation and Web site — is designed to bridge gaps he's found in the medical system.

Most diseases have their own advocacy groups that focus only on that illness, he says. The National Institutes of Health, often the guiding hand in deciding which illnesses get the most attention, are fractured and devote relatively little to autoim-

mune disorders, Henderson feels.

"I just want my fair share," Henderson says.

But he, TePastte and others have come to the conclusion that cures for autoimmune disease will rest with genetic engineering like that done by UAB's J. Edwin Blalock, who is working on a genetic-based vaccine.

All autoimmune illnesses should be looked at together, Henderson says.

"The treatments are very similar and the cures, when they come, will be applicable to all autoimmune diseases," he predicts. "If we find the cure for one, it may be the golden key for all autoimmune disorders."

The proceeds from Henderson's book all will go to the foundation, the Birmingham-based International Autoimmune Disease Research Foundation. It will be run by a board of directors, and a board of scientists will help review grant applications on promising research.

Henderson plans to use the book as a calling card to approach philanthropists and foundations to help fund the autoimmune work.

Today, Henderson maintains about the same energy level he had at the peak of his life as a physician and businessman. He rests in the morning before a meeting and takes a short nap in the afternoon if he plans to go out.

He works out each morning, watches his diet, makes it a point to call family and friends, takes his medicine and is careful to maintain a balance among his endeavors.

Henderson expects to have another crisis phase of his illness, so he's taking advantage of the remission now to spread the word about autoimmune disorders and chronic illness.

"He tries to keep his wheel well-rounded and no one spoke longer than the other," Beth Henderson notes, with an amused smile on her face as she watches him talk.

"If you let one get longer than the others," Ron Henderson adds, "your wheel keeps bumping through life."

And that makes getting over the next mountain a lot harder than it has to be.

DOZEN:
You're in charge of your life

From Page 1E

▶ **Minimize and manage the stress in your life.** You cannot eliminate it all, Henderson notes. But stress alters and perhaps weakens your immune system, leaving your body at risk.

▶ **Don't focus on your chronological age.** Don't deny it, either, but view your age as a positive and keep moving forward.

▶ **Don't isolate yourself.** Isolation is brutal, and you may be tempted not to call family and friends, or make the effort to see them, because you don't feel well. Make the effort, he says.

▶ **Don't stop looking for solutions to problems.** Henderson says this may be his strongest recommendation. Don't become

complacent, he says. Be aggressive.

▶ **Accept your chronic disease as a part of your life** rather than focus on it as a barrier to getting the most out of life. Your illness is only one part of your life, Henderson says. It may dictate certain details of your activities, but by focusing elsewhere, you will be happier and more productive.

▶ **Attempt to find mental, emotional and spiritual comfort through prayer, meditation, reading and discussing your needs openly with family, friends and clergy.** You should intellectually reach out to family and friends. Spiritually, he says, you need to find the path that best suits you.

From "Attacking Myasthenia Gravis: A Key in the Battle Against Autoimmune Diseases" (Court Street Press, $25.95).

The Birmingham News, 2002. *(continued from page 150)*

FOUNDATION Digest

JOIN THE PARTY OF THE CENTURY!

It's a party 100 years in the making.

St. Vincent's Centennial Gala takes place November 7, 100 years to the month after the first four Daughters of Charity came to Birmingham and treated their first patients in a Southside mansion they had converted into a hospital.

One of the centerpieces of the Centennial Celebration, the Gala, will mark this momentous anniversary and extend St. Vincent's mission to the community by benefitting a new lodging facility for families of patients with special needs (see story on page 6).

The black tie affair will be held in a deluxe event tent on the lawn in front of the new Bruno Conference Center on the hospital campus.

Co-chairs of the Gala are **Dr. and Mrs. Merrill Bradley** and **Mr. and Mrs. Stanley Mackin.**

Dinner will be by **Chef Chris Hastings** of Hot and Hot Fish Club. Hastings was recently named one of the Best Regional Chefs by the Mondavi Winery. After-dinner dancing will be to the music of **Al Belletto's New Orleans Jazz Band**, featuring vocalist **Leif Pedersen.**

Tickets to the Gala are $250 per person with sponsored tables beginning at $2,000.

Photographed at the Gala preview party on July 30 are, from top left, 1) Mr. and Mrs. Stanley Mackin with Dr. and Mrs. Rex Harris, 2) Chef Chris Hastings of Hot and Hot Fish Club, 3) Dr. Ronald Henderson, Nina Botsford and Wayne Gillis, and 4) Leif Pedersen and jazz band members.

CENTENNIAL
1898 ~ 1998
St. Vincent's Foundation

St. Vincent's Foundation Digest, 1998. *(continued from page 179)*

Submitted Progress

From left are: Beth Ann Henderson, Dr. Ronald Henderson and Mal Moore, the athletics director at the University of Alabama.

Former Autauga County Lion makes donation to U of A

By Jimmy White
Progress writer

Dr. Ronald E. Henderson, a native of Prattville, gave back to the University of Alabama in ceremonies held at the Bryant Hall on the grounds of the campus. In ceremonies held Sept. 8, Henderson presented the University with $250,000 for a Guest Suite at the University's Bryant Hall Academic Center. The gift matched his Prattville classmate, Joe Chambliss' gift of the same amount, for a guest suite.

The two guest suites are approximately 1,900 square feet and are used primarily by the University for overnight stays for dignitaries and special guests. A 1955 graduate of Autauga County High School, Henderson has been a medical leader and entrepreneur for three and half decades in Birmingham,

after graduating from the University's Medial College in 1962.

He is currently teaching at the University's School of Medical School in Birmingham. He is also active in a number of state and national organizations. Henderson was an OB-GYN specialist and founded the Henderson and Walton Women's Center in Birmingham, as well as a health maintenance organization.

After attending a November 2005 ceremony at Bryant Hall where his classmate at Autauga County High School, Joe Chambliss, gave $250,000 to the University's Crimson Foundation and a suite at Bryant Hall was named for the Chambliss Family, Henderson said he wanted to do something for the school.

"I had heard Dr. (Robert) Witt, the President of the University speak at the Birmingham Downtown Rotary Club about

the University going after the best and brightest and increasing the GPA of all students, including our student -athletes. My wife, Beth, and I had been looking for a way to give back to the University for all it had given us through the years. After hearing Dr. Witt and his vision for our campus, we wanted to help in any way we could. Then, seeing how my friend Joe Chambliss was able to help the athletic department convinced me to do he same thing."

Ronald Henderson grew up in Prattville, and played tight end for the Autauga County Lions. He played under the legendary Fred Jensen, lettering three seasons in three sports. He married his childhood sweetheart Beth Ann Summerville. They have two daughters, Dr. Rhonda H. Powell and Ellen H. Dover, and one son, William E. Henderson, and four grandchildren.

The Prattville Progress, September 2006. *(continued from page 179)*

Centennial Lodge, revisited:
Dr. Ron and Beth Henderson extend their torch-bearing legacy cont.

"Hospitality is taken from the same word as 'hospital,'" noted Wayne Carmello-Harper, St. Vincent's Health System Senior Vice President of Mission Integration and Chief Philanthropy Officer. "Our entire ministry is dedicated to bringing this experience to those who turn to us in times of medical need. We are deeply grateful to Ron and Beth for revitalizing the Lodge, which is aligned with our commitment to person-centered care."

Henderson is a member of the Alabama Healthcare Hall of Fame, a former professor of medicine at the University of Alabama School of Medicine at the University of Alabama at Birmingham, the founder of Henderson & Walton, and founder or co-founder of three other health-related firms. He is an emeritus board member of St. Vincent's Foundation as well as having served on multiple other boards, including Alabama's State Committee of Public Health.

"I've had quite a career. So, we hope this commitment to the Lodge will comply with what the Daughters of Charity insisted on—that our commitment to excellence should extend not only to St. Vincent's level of care, but to its facilities as well."

Only in this country

For those familiar with local donors and volunteer leadership, Dr. Ron and Beth Henderson are known as consistently generous St. Vincent's supporters. Although this physician has contributed expertise and monetary gifts to multiple St. Vincent's projects and committees, the Lodge renewal has special meaning for him.

"I am a tenant farmer's son," said Henderson. "What I have experienced in my career could only happen in this country. I've had a lot of mentors along the way, from the people who helped me get into college to all the supporters I've had since."

Henderson has therefore devoted his career and retirement to returning that support. The renovation and renaming of Centennial Lodge will serve as a fitting reminder of what helping others "along the way" can do, not only for one individual, but for all those whose lives will be touched in decades to come.

Honorariums *The following individuals were recognized through a gift in their honor.*

Stephen M. Anderson	Beverly Golightly	Jennifer Manasco	Cindy L. Rhodes
Dr. Joaquin Arciniegas	Samuel G. Grainger	Michelle L. McMullen	Dr. Susan P. Salter
Dr. Cara Bondly	Dr. William C. Hays III	Sr. Brenda Monahan, D.C.	Dr. Sally P. Salter
Bruno Cancer Center Staff	Diane Hill	Susan R. Moon	St. Vincent's Birmingham Gift
Katherine W. Buchwald	Valerie G. Holman	William M. Moran	Shop and Book Store
Dr. Gray C. Buck III	Natalie Hooks	Stephen H. Njoroge	Dr. William J. Tapscott
Wayne Carmello-Harper	Suzanne R. Hoye	Dr. Gerald P. Norris	Brian H. Thorn
Eva Davey	Denise B. Johnson	Lee Patterson	Timothy Tucker
Bernie Favara	Louis Josof	Dr. John A. Piede	Dr. Joseph E. Welden, Jr.
Dr. Philip J. Fischer	Jackie Kennedy	Jim Powell	Sr. Dinah White, D.C.
Dr. James A. Flanagan	Virginia S. Ladd	Dr. David L. Rader	
Barry Godby	John Laliberte	Angela Ray	

2

The Vigil Newsletter, St. Vincent's Foundation, Spring 2015. (continued from page 180)

APPENDIX C

RESOURCES

A new map of Alabama with its roads & distances from place to place along the stage & steam boat routes, published by S. Augustus Mitchell (1846). Courtesy of the Birmingham Public Library, Birmingham, Alabama.

Articles and newsletters reprinted with permission of: *The Birmingham News,* Landov Media, New York, NY; *The Birmingham Business Journal,* Quality Resource Group, Plymouth, MN; *The Prattville Progress,* Pars International, New York, NY; The Medical Association of Alabama; St. Vincent's Foundation; and the Alabama Farmer's Federation.

Ronald E. Henderson, M.D., *The Woman I Am, A Woman's Guide To Health, Happiness, and Success in the 1990s, The Physicians of Henderson & Walton Women's Center,* as told to Anita Smith, Twin Valley Press, Montgomery, Alabama, 1992.

Ronald E. Henderson, M.D., *Attacking Myasthenia Gravis: A Key in the Battle Against Autoimmune Diseases,* Court Street Press, Montgomery, Alabama, 2003.

William McDonald, *Wadsworth Flat: The Story of Three Remarkable Brothers,* Photography by William McDonald. Twin Valley Press, Montgomery, Alabama, 1983.

UAB Archives: scans made November 2014 for Haden Holmes Brown for use in a forthcoming privately funded and distributed publication she is compiling for Ronald E. Henderson, MD. All rights retained. These images may only be used for the Henderson publication noted above and may not be reused for other purposes and should not be shared. Anyone wishing to obtain copies of these images should contact the UAB Archives at 205-934-1896.

Joe and Ron, 2014.

FOR CURLY EARL

With gratitude and a deep devotion to my best friend, I offer my collection of loving thoughts of our bonding since childhood and over the years.

Ron's heart and soul is best portrayed through a most noble philosophy of life: "Success is the progressive realization of worthy ideals." Ron has demonstrated without waver an indefatigable desire to reach out to his fellow man, whether through medicine, business, church, or community. His indomitable spirit casts shrouds of love over all elements of his life. How is it that one could not love and admire this family man of noble deeds?

Ron's life has been dedicated to aspiring to be all that one can be while achieving the same. He has persevered in spite of humble beginnings, personal health issues, and the hard knocks that life brings to all of us. A living testimony to his love of people has manifested itself over the years through his commitment to Autauga High School Class of '55, our 60th year reunion this coming year. His offer of his beloved farm in our hometown of Prattville, Alabama, to host the class reunion speaks volumes about his legacy of caring and sharing.

To summarize my feelings for my lifetime buddy, I quote the writer Earl Nightingale: Ron's "service to humanity has been his best work in life."

—Little Joe of Prattville

ABOUT THE AUTHOR

RONALD E. HENDERSON, MD

"Ron has demonstrated an indefatigable desire to reach out to his fellow man, whether through medicine, business, church or community."

—Joe Chambliss, *chairman of the board and CEO of Florida Turnpike Services, and managing general partner of the Chambliss Group*

"Many businesspeople are so worried about making a wrong decision that they end up paralyzed and make no decision at all. Ron's process is just the opposite of that— he efficiently thinks through the elements of a decision, decides, and never looks back to second-guess himself."

—George B. Salem, *chairman and president of GBS Ventures, Inc., and chairman/CEO of ProxsysRx*

"Ron Henderson is a 'hard dog to keep under the porch.' His impact on the practice of medicine is huge in Birmingham and Alabama, and for that matter, the nation. Always one step ahead of the rest of us in innovation, he is my role model for how to think out of the box and move boldly."

—Edward E. Partridge, MD, *director, Comprehensive Cancer Center, professor of gynecologic oncology, Evalina B. Spencer chair in oncology, University of Alabama at Birmingham*

RONALD E. HENDERSON, physician, entrepreneur, and author, and his wife, Beth, divide their time between Mountain Brook, Alabama, and their farm in Prattville. Henderson wrote the book *Attacking Myasthenia Gravis: A Key in the Battle Against Autoimmune Diseases* and contributed to the book *The Woman I Am, A Woman's Guide To Health, Happiness, and Success in the 1990s.*

Beginning in 1968, Henderson spent twenty-six years in private practice in Birmingham, Alabama, ultimately founding the Henderson & Walton Women's Center at St. Vincent's Hospital. A highly motivated entrepreneur, he also founded a practice management company, the Southeast's first physician-owned HMO, a physician-owned and -operated liability insurance company, and the Southeast's first stand-alone surgical center.

Currently, Henderson is a consultant for private medical businesses and St. Vincent's Hospital.

PHOTOGRAPH ABOVE BY KATHERINE HENDERSON